To Dr. Marable

It is with great pleasure that I present Black to the Future. Enjoy this journey and know that I truly appreciate your support.

Thanks again
and
God Bless

Peter W. Brownell

BLACK TO THE FUTURE

From the Plantation to the Corporation

BLACK TO THE FUTURE

From the Plantation to the Corporation

A Socio-Economic / Historic-Theologic thesis on the irreparable damage The House Negro and their so-called leaders have inflicted upon the Black Race

By

Peter W. Sherrill

(The Last Plaintiff standing in the Texaco Racial Discrimination Fiasco)

The Untold Story

ISBN: 978-0-9816838-0-5

Printed in the United States
By
Lightning Source Inc.
1246 Heil Quaker Blvd.
LaVergne, Tennessee
37086

Acknowledgments

I dedicate this book to my mother, my strongest supporter, who was diagnosed with uterine cancer in its final stages, while I was in the primary stages of editing this work, who passed away, July 19, 2006 at 2:30 pm. How I truly wished she were here to see this literary work published. I Love You.

I also dedicate this book to Sil Chambers, the silent lead plaintiff who died shortly after the lawsuit was won. Only in his early forties at the time, he endured the rigors and constant demands, the challenges and continuous criticism subsequent to the Texaco Racial Discrimination Lawsuit. No, he didn't have the opportunity to write a book as did the other lead plaintiff and/or share the spotlight with the so-called Black Leaders, who were nowhere to be found until after it was over, but I say to him Rest in Peace for the truth has finally been told.

And last but not least, to my two children, Imani and Amari Sherrill, ages eleven and nine respectively, my two biggest fans, who really helped me keep this clean. I love you with all my heart.

And a special thanks to Elsa Forsythe and Lynne Goodman, your assistance was paramount to the completion of this literary work.

CONTENTS

Chapter 1
Mission Accomplished

Lights, cameras, action! There they were, all the so-called Black leaders expressing their outrage about the "Texaco Tapes," Corporate Executives calling us everything from *niggas* to porch monkeys, and the infamous "black jelly beans" – God only knows what else they were calling us in those private meetings. We never were privy to that information. I understand that there were several tapes that had all kinds of derogatory remarks about us.

Yeah, we had Texaco right where we wanted them, and all this right in the midst of a Class Action lawsuit by African Americans. However, this is only the beginning about this sorry, pathetic, disgraceful, spineless class of individuals you could ever imagine, and I don't mean the Texaco executives, even though the shoe fits. I know because I was there, front and center, on the battlefield, in the halls of the once great Corporate World Headquarters of Texaco Inc.

So, let's go back, "Black to the Future" to the how, where, when and why this all started.

"We won, we won! The CEO settled." I know exactly how George must have felt when he thought the war against Iraq was all wrapped up, only to find out that the real war was just about to begin. So much for "mission accomplished." All those *House Negroes* who sat on the sidelines during this whole ordeal were now rejoicing like they did something of importance, while a few of us put our necks on the line. What a bunch of cowards. It still angers me, even to this day. I was glad the war was just beginning. Actually, if it wasn't for the war, my role wouldn't have been as significant, because it was the backlash that catapulted me into the spotlight. However, I would still have been able to write the true and untold story about this fiasco they called a Class Action lawsuit against Texaco. It surely wasn't any thanks to those so-called leaders that weren't anywhere to be found while we were actually fighting this Goliath of Corporate America. So where were all of our so-called leaders before the cameras? I'll tell you where! Nowhere! Nowhere, at all to be found! All of a sudden they came marching up to Texaco after the fact, like some knight in shining armor. Hell, we didn't need them now, for what? Those self-serving opportunistic sell-outs, for lack of a better word, cause my dear sweet mother, and young daughter want to read this book. Actually, now that my dear sweet mother has past from cancer, in the editing phase of this manuscript, I just may tell it exactly like it is and like it was. Those god-damn *niggas* who sat there for all those years and said nothing are garbage, as I will reveal throughout this book. There are a lot of expletives I want to use, but I am trying hard to restrain myself from writing them, so forgive me if in the passion of my writing I call them what they truly are. Please forgive me. You must realize that I really have pure contempt for these individuals, and they really annoy me. No wonder we can't get "nowhere" of any significance in this country. Sure one or two have been incorporated into the scheme of things, mainly to pacify any outcries of inclusiveness, but our leaders, excuse me, so-called leaders, don't even deserve any respect, and guess what, they aren't respected.

Those *House Negroes* are killing us. Actually they are selling us out, just like they did during the slave trade and back on the plantation during slavery.

I have this theory, and it's sort of based on that old saying, "the apple don't fall far from the tree." I bet any amount of money that if you trace those *House Negroes'* lineage, you'll probably find that they come from the same line of Africans who sold their brothers and sisters into slavery! Surely they are a disgrace to our race, just like the idiots who sold us in the first place.

So, what really happened at Texaco that led up to this classless Class Action lawsuit?

I remember being a temp delivering boxes at the Corporate World Headquarters at Texaco. Yeah, I had a degree, but I also had a family, and as far as I was concerned this was just a pit stop until I got the call from the Fire Department to become a Firefighter. When the call never came, I viewed this as a great opportunity and a great story of starting from the bottom and working my way up through the ranks in Corporate America. What I later found out was that not only was there a glass ceiling but it was reinforced with cement. However, that didn't bother me as much as when I remember how many of those individuals who were Black like me, would avoid speaking to me, like I was less than a person because I delivered boxes. Yet, the whites never made me feel any less of an employee. As I think about it, I might have just been viewed as a good *House Negro* who understood his place in the halls of Corporate America. Even though

I have a degree, I will tell you one thing I did learn from the time I graduated and began working, whites don't give a damn what kind of degree a *nigga* has, you still a *nigga*. After working temp in a few companies, I really thought Texaco was different.

Soon I went from being a temp delivering boxes to an employee they created a position for. Wow, what a great company! I'm on my way. So I thought. I bought my first car, brand new Nissan Maxima. My fiancée, who worked for General Foods, purchased a townhouse now that I had a steady job in a major Fortune 500 Corporation. Life was great. And guess what, all of a sudden those *House Negroes* who wouldn't even acknowledge I existed, began speaking to me. I was wearing new clothes and soon new suits, not like I didn't have suits in my wardrobe before, but now I was viewed differently. Allegedly I was respected, and when they found out I had a degree, I was allegedly even more acceptable. I would like to take a moment to tell all those pathetic *House Negroes* who treated me like I didn't exist while I was delivering boxes at Texaco, to go straight to Hell. I'll never be like you. Nor do I, or did I ever want or need to be accepted by you to feel validated or substantiated.

As you can tell, I have pure contempt for these types of individuals. Also, interestingly enough, you don't only find these pathetic individuals on the plantations of Corporate America, but also in the congregations of all the Black Churches, those so-called puritanical Christians. They sit in the front pews at church and praise the Lord on Sunday and by Monday they are selling their souls to the first bidder.

Remember this, I'm not by any means proclaiming to be some sanctimonious individual, but I ain't no sell-out. Never was and never will be. I owe my soul to no one.

Soon there was another promotion. Now my fiancée actually wants to marry me. Interesting! Actually, it's a sad story of how we treat one another in our relationships. There was a time when black women stood by our sides through thick and thin, but now that they make more money than most Black men, 'forget about it.' However, that's by design and our women don't even see it, or refuse to see it. Black women need to recognize what is happening in this game. I will say this, the Black woman is not excluded from selling us out either. Actually, they have become some of the biggest culprits.

There were two gentlemen, dare I say White, (well we know in Texaco they couldn't have been Black, because there weren't any Blacks in any type of position to help anybody, yet alone themselves), who were very instrumental in my becoming a permanent employee. They created a position for me, gave me my two years temp time as time served, which they didn't have to do, who really looked out for me for whatever the reason might have been. To them I am grateful and I didn't even have to sell my soul, even though when they retired things began to change. Thus began my understanding of the systemic discriminatory process practiced at Texaco.

What many people don't know is that there was a prior attempt to sue Texaco for discrimination before this Class Action suit, by a group of individuals, of which one was an attorney for the company. And don't you know, one of those *House Negroes* went back and told "*massa*," and the attorney was fired. That's what I'm talking about, the irreparable damage these *House Negroes* can cause. Now I may not be able to prove it was one of those useless sell-outs, but if the shoe fits! This lawsuit was pursued with such discretion that it had to be someone they trusted, or someone who was acting like they were down with the cause then turned around and blew the whistle. You remember how it used to be back on the plantation when the *House Negro* would find out about a plan to escape from the plantation and run straight to *massa* and give the date, time, who, and every bit of information he could think of. This is what I'm talking about. I already know that slavery was horrible, I already know that Whites really don't like Blacks, but it's these kinds of acts of ignorance perpetrated by us upon us, like black on black crime, that I believe have hindered us more than, or just as much as racism and the prolonged agony of slavery. You know, as long as we feel that we are better than our brother or sister because we have, lets say a better position in a company, or because we live in a better neighborhood than our brother or sister, we will continue to fuel the mentality that made those same *House Negroes* feel they were too good to acknowledge an individual delivering boxes so he could support his family. Hell, it's an honest living! As long as our young women glorify the drug dealer instead of that hard working brother making an honest living, who can't afford that fancy ride like the drug dealer, we will continue to have these problems. Come to think of it, there really

6

isn't much difference between the *House Negro*, and the individuals who admire drug dealers. The House Negro admires anyone because of their money and material status, while the drug dealer is admired for the same reasons. Whatever happened to being the best street sweeper? Whatever happened to whatever you do, be the best? Are we so caught up in this status game that we forget that we still don't have anything of real value in the grand scheme of this society? And although some have benefited, the majority of our race is still in despair. Those who have benefited really don't give a damn about their people still in the struggle. What they don't realize, but better soon realize, is that with all this right-sizing and mergers going on, they can easily become the next victims as many were about to find out after this Class Action lawsuit. They thought that because they were good *House Negroes* and didn't participate in the lawsuit, they would be spared the wrath of *massa*. What they seem to have forgotten is that when *massa* goes on a rampage against his slaves for disobedience, he takes his vengeance out on everyone. They probably don't even know anything about what happened in Tulsa Oklahoma, or Charleston South Carolina when they burned and tried to kill everyone in the whole damn town. I knew it was coming, however, I really didn't care what was about to happen to those *useless, parasitical, bastards*, who sat there at Texaco for twenty or more years, happy as a pig in shit!

Chapter 2

The System and The Lawsuit

The two gentlemen who helped me have now retired, so I have to start all over again, so to speak. But it's not so bad. I still have the relationships I have developed, from the time when I delivered boxes. However, there is a small detail that has emerged about the system of promotions and pay grades. In order to understand the systemic discriminatory practices that existed at Texaco, you must understand pay grade levels and promotions to understand how this game is played. The pay grades start as low as Level 3 and go as high as Level 35. So here I am at Level 5/6, but with an opportunity here and there everything should be just fine, or so I thought. There's just one catch in this system. You can only post for a promotion two pay grades above where you are, and then you can't post again for another position for two years. I believe it's two. So here's the math. My supervisor retired at pay grade 15, so first of all I couldn't even replace him, regardless of the fact that I had a degree in Management and Economics, because it was 9 grades above my current grade and you can only post two grades at a time. Those are the rules. So I began to calculate how long would it take to get to Grade 15 from Grade level 6. Two grades to Grade 8, then two years to Grade 10 for two years, then Grade 12 for two years, then Grade 14 for two years. So it would take approximately 8 years to reach Grade 15, if all went well. Remember, the highest-grade level is 35. I didn't even do that math. My American dream about rising through the ranks of

Corporate America was fading fast. After five years with the company, with good reviews, I finally decided to voice my concern regarding my future. I addressed these concerns in a memo to the Head of my department; after all he had arranged my photo shoot with Roger Staubach and then had it autographed for me. What a great guy! For those who don't know, Roger Staubach is the Hall of Fame Quarterback who used to play for the Dallas Cowboys football team. So, me and my Department Head met, had a discussion and I got the 'pep talk' and all that, and still nothing. I wrote another memo, and then they moved me to the Financial Planning Group. Great, right? However, the move was lateral. Ain't that some real bullshit! Thus came my first enquiry about the lawsuit. But before that occurred I was promised a two-grade promotion by my supervisor's replacement, and when it came time for my review and he told me some garbage about grade levels not meaning that much, that's when I wrote my first letter to the EEOC. This *white mother fucka* either thought I was stupid, or thought I was stupid. Hell, grade levels meant everything in this game. I wouldn't have known that if my supervisor hadn't retired. I was totally oblivious to the rules that governed this game. Once I became aware of how the game was played, everything changed. One thing you don't do to me and think that you are not going to have to deal with me is to insult my intelligence. Another thing, I am always skeptical of, is when people praise someone they don't even know. I guess it goes back to admiring people for all the wrong reasons. All those *House Negroes*

9

were raving about this new gentleman who had been hired as EEOC and how I should meet with him. I never trusted those *House Negroes*, however I sent him a memo, and we soon met. One side note, I became famous for writing memos. As I listened to him tell me I need to dress better and invest in some white shirts and ties, etc., I smiled, as I purposely dressed moderate for the meeting. He tried desperately to defend my new supervisor, and that let me know he was full of garbage also. Then he went on to tell me, "You shouldn't go around mentioning that you have a Degree in Management and Economics," and that I shouldn't have taken the position that they created for me. I said to myself, "This *nigga* must be crazy." Then he went on to tell me, "you don't want to be known as a troublemaker." So now I'm a troublemaker, might as well cause some trouble. I go to my boy, who was a true renegade fighting this hypocrisy and double standard in this company, never biting his tongue and always telling it just like it is. "Give me the number," I say to him. He says, "What happened, man?" "Just give me the damn number." Of course he gave me the number, then he followed with "I told you, they weren't going to give you no two pay grades." "Give me the number," I reiterated.

I remember how he used to laugh at me when I used to tell him, "One day we are going to be running this company." Being a 10 plus year vet, and myself still wet behind the ears, he used to laugh. I was serious, because that was the American dream, or so I thought. But it is, isn't it? Or am I that naïve? Isn't it about dreaming the impossible dream? I used to love that song, To Dream the Impossible Dream. Was that not meant for us? Now that I remember, that song wasn't taught to me until I transferred from my neighborhood school on the Black side of town to the White school across town in third grade. Interesting!

Anyway, I made the phone call to these attorneys in Washington D.C. who had decided to take the case of Racial Discrimination against Texaco. I spoke with this young lady; I say that because I am not sure how old she was. Anyway, I told her my situation in the company and she listened, then she kindly informed me that this lawsuit "isn't for people like you." "What do you mean, people like me?" It's for Blacks ain't it? "Yes, but it's for the 'Professional Blacks,'" those few Blacks who were in pay grades 16 and above. Those damn *House Negroes*! Selling us out again! Mind you, the highest *House Negro* was maybe a Grade 18. My point is that the majority of Blacks in the company were below grade level 9, with maybe a level 10 here and there, but for all intents and purposes, we were at the bottom of the pay grades.

I said, "I have a Degree in Management and Economics and I am a professional." Then she kindly told me she understood, and that maybe if they didn't have success in arbitration, they may have to look into going Class Action. This was amazing! A discrimination lawsuit that eliminates most of the people it's filing discrimination for. Isn't that reprehensible. Maybe now you can begin to see why I call this Class Action Lawsuit a fiasco. I couldn't believe my ears.

All this time my boy was telling me my case would be great, with my degree and all. And I kept telling him that Texaco hadn't done anything at the time to warrant me joining this suit, until I was lied to about my promotion. Well, I literally cursed him out the next day. But imagine, what kind of lawsuit was this? Just for a select few who were having problems with the company. Not to say they were not justified, but they didn't give a damn about the majority of us. Case and point. Now you tell me if that isn't reprehensible, totally disgusting and disgraceful? Actually, it's some straight up bullshit!

So that is how the lawsuit of racial discrimination resurfaced. Remember, there had already been one attempt and the only Black lawyer for the company was fired. The lead plaintiff, or the woman who eventually became the lead plaintiff and filed this grievance, did it for one reason. She was informed that her name had been removed from the 'fast track' list. Texaco had vehemently denied the existence of such a list, until somehow, the list was produced. In some regards I do understand how she could feel betrayed, because it was that same kind of betrayal that caused me to seek to join this lawsuit. After all, Texaco begged her to come to the Corporate Headquarters in White Plains, NY. Prior to her arrival, she was Vice President at a Chase Bank, from what I understood, and Texaco was desperately seeking someone to showcase to quiet some of its critics regarding the lack of African Americans in any Senior Level position in this Global Company. Let me tell you, there were no Blacks in Middle Management or any positions of Management throughout the whole company, except for two supervisors; you guessed it, one in Shipping and the other in the Mail Room. One's status was based upon how many windows your office had. I learned that from my friend, who taught me the ropes while I was in Shipping and Receiving. Realize that Texaco Corporate Headquarters was three football fields long, and one football field wide, an impressive structure second only to the corporation that my fiancée worked at, known as the Taj Mahal of Corporate America, down the strip, owned by Philip Morris. Every day was a workout delivering supplies to all the departments throughout the building. But that is how I became so popular in the building. I delivered supplies with style, a smile and with dignity. I was going to be the best damn delivery person of supplies ever. I was also very glad to be a part of this organization because I knew that someday, someway, somehow, somewhere along the line, an opportunity would manifest itself in this great organization. It saddens me that this beautifully manicured and maintained facility was beginning to exude the stench of a plantation. I guess that's why those *House Negroes* sat around for so long and never said a word. They were probably feeling like "we gotta good *massa*". And you know what? They did have a good '*massa*". They were so glad just to be there, pretending when they go home to have some important position at the Corporate World Headquarters of this Fortune 500 Company. I admit, before I sought real upward mobility in this organization I didn't pretend to have an important position, however, I did like the sound of telling professional women I worked at The

Corporate World Headquarters of Texaco Inc., especially when I was no longer delivering boxes. Hell, they thought I was important, and that's all that mattered at that time.   Yeah I admit it. I used the Texaco name to impress women. However, on the other hand that shows how shallow their mentality was. I mean, that would be the first question out of their mouth, who do you work for, and when I would say The Corporate World Headquarters of Texaco Inc., I was in, if you know what I mean. Hell, when I used to tell women that I was a college graduate but just working temp, or looking for a job, I was getting nowhere. Personally I think it's a sad account of what Black relationships have been reduced to, but enough of that for now.

 Anyway, arbitration was getting nowhere, so the select few and the attorneys decided to pursue Class Action. That's when I got the call. "Oh, now you want me to join the lawsuit?" I guess you can figure out what my first response was, or at least what I was thinking. Now, my story was the perfect example of that systemic racism that was being instituted at Texaco. To some degree it really was. Still floundering at Grade Level 6, barely making $25,000 a year, in the late nineties with a four-year degree. People would always say to me you should leave and go somewhere else and make more money. But what they didn't realize was it wasn't all about the money. I had an old wise professor who told us in class one day that money shouldn't be the primary reason to join a company. I knew one day, that if I stayed, and paid my dues, that doors would open up in Texaco. Unfortunately, before that happened, Texaco caught the entire wrath of my indignation from all the humiliation I suffered in Corporate America from the time I graduated from college in 1980. I remember working for $4.88 an hour at Loral Electronics and $5.00 an hour in Lower Manhattan at Morgan Guarantee and Trust. 1980, the year when 'good ole boy' Ronald Reagan became President of this country. There was a backlash throughout this whole country to make things like they used to be before all this Affirmative Action and equality. Employment for Blacks, college educated or not, was strictly entry level everywhere, if anywhere. I venture to guess that '*massa*' was fed-up with those damn *House Negroes* crossing over and having their way with his women during the sixties and seventies, and I guess when Jesse decided to run for President they said this has got to stop. Whatever the reasons, Black unemployment was definitely on the rise and we still remain the highest unemployed Race even today. So when I joined this lawsuit and gave my deposition, anyone who wronged me caught it. The EEOC who told me to dress better, and that I shouldn't go around mentioning my degree, etc. My Black female supervisor when I was laterally moved into the Financial Planning Group who gave me the worst evaluation ever, the head of the Financial Planning group, the Head of the Corporate Services Department, and Texaco. I will say this much, I didn't discriminate. If you were Black and crossed me I let you have it with the same indignation as with the Whites.

Interestingly enough, however, my story was by no means as horrific as some of the depositions I read. In Houston they were catching real hell. Pure unadulterated racism. That dirty South I know so well, especially after going to college in Florida. Blacks there wouldn't even look White people in the eyes when speaking. Damn, I was like, "Where the hell am I? Is this America?" I actually went through 'Culture Shock' in Florida. Let me tell you something else, when I went to Houston, Texas for the first time in my life while employed at Texaco it proved to be just as interesting. Racism is a real ugly thing. And once being racially discriminated against, the scars never go away. Or do they? They shouldn't. We need to be reminded of the horrors inflicted upon us and say like others, never again, never again. Hell, they are still persecuting war criminals from W.W. II who are almost ready to die. We should learn from this and hold those benefactors from our enslavement accountable, but I don't know if we will ever be able to do that because we have so many damn *House Negroes* willing to sell their souls to live next door to them.

Chapter 3

The Deposition

Everyone (meaning the plaintiffs) at Corporate Headquarters was excited when it was time for me to give my deposition. Yeah, somehow the cornerstone that was rejected had become the main cornerstone. Something like that I read in the Bible. You "good ole Christians" know what I am talking about. Yeah, I bet you do.

I had never given a 'dep' before and I wasn't sure what to expect. If there was any doubt that I was part of this Action it was all about to be put on the table now. I felt like this star witness or something. Now, all of a sudden, I am privy to updates and things. Even though I still can't dismiss the fact that this Lawsuit wasn't meant for 'people like me.' I also can't disregard the fact that it was these same people, the lead plaintiffs, who acted like I didn't exist while I was delivering boxes. Hell, one of them wouldn't speak to no- one Black if they weren't part of the select Blacks in the Company. I was shocked the day she actually spoke to me in the cafeteria, after I became this star witness so to speak. This is what I am talking about. This is the mentality that is really commonplace among Blacks in this country, from the time they were allowed to be in the house on the plantation, up to being a supervisor in the Mailroom in the corporation. They don't give a damn about nobody unless they have some type of status or recognition. Regardless of these feelings of conflict, I knew that this was something I really had to do in spite of those pathetic Negroes. Yeah that's right, those pathetic Negroes, who would make sure, now that it was known that I was part of this Lawsuit, to stay as far away from me as possible. When in close proximity, they use to say, "causing any trouble?" or "watch out here comes trouble." I would like to take the time out here to say to those pathetic ass *House Negroes* that they can all go to hell. That's not what I really wanted to say but my daughter really wants to read this book. I remember telling my daughter that I was going to write a clean copy and a raw version like they do in rap. She was in shock. She is now eleven, so I have to be careful what I say, I guess, but I might just let it rip, because there are some matters that really truly piss me the "F" off. Ah, I feel a little better now. I do have to let this go after carrying it for so long. You know when they say that once in your life you need to stand up for something, it is really true. I mean, after I joined this cause, this righteous cause, against this Goliath of Corporate America, I was proud of what I was doing. I'll tell you something else, if you don't believe in God before you do something like this, you sure will during and after. I began reading my Psalms again every day. There really was a war going on at Texaco. Every morning I would bench-press 250 lbs. before I would go to work, ready for battle, and run 5 miles every afternoon. There was no room for the weak. There was no room for those pathetic *House Negroes*. You may not understand why I am calling them pathetic now but just wait till you read some of the things that transpired later on during this Class Action Lawsuit. Some of them need to be shot, no, how about castrated, that should make them feel back at home on the plantation, those pathetic, complacent, docile and useless bastards. When you take the time out to think back to the brutality inflicted upon our race by White America, and they were really barbaric, why would anyone continue to strive to emulate their way of life? Anyway, I get the call to go give my deposition at some law office in Midtown Manhattan. It's show time but this is the truth, the whole truth and nothing but. So the questioning begins. He finally ends by asking me why do I feel like I've been discriminated against. I reply, something to the effect, "do you think that if I was White and had a Bachelor's degree, I be going through this?" Remember, I was at a grade level that was for someone in the mailroom or something. Later I found out that the majority of the Blacks in the company were stuck at the bottom like the reference that was made about us as "black jelly beans" being stuck to the bottom of the jar. Ultimately that became my famous quote, which was showcased in the Journal Newspaper's Sunday edition. "Show me one white male with a degree plus a double major in Management and Economics in this company at a grade level six, barely making $25,000 a year. Show me one. Just one. Realize there weren't any whites with or without a degree making a mere $25,000 at Headquarters. I never knew why I majored in Economics, but I am damn glad I did, because it took every bit of economic savvy I could apply to survive after graduating from college. In essence the salary didn't really bother me. I just looked at it as a challenge. Remember, I was working for $4.88 an hour at Loral Electronics, a Fortune 500 company and as a temp at Morgan Guarantee and Trust for $5.00 an hour and was making ends meet. So this was nothing compared to where I had previously been. Actually it was a piece a cake financially. It was the thought that I was Black, the color of my skin was the primary reason myself and everyone else in this Company were at the level they were. It's a shame. It was disgraceful, yet Texaco didn't feel that there was anything wrong and was not about to budge on its position on this Class Action Lawsuit. You know it was that same arrogance that sent Texaco into bankruptcy with that 12 billion lawsuit won by Getty Oil. They thought because they were Texaco and Getty was this small fish they didn't stand a chance against Texaco, the Goliath of Corporate America. Well for those who remember, that really cost them. It was beginning to look like we were on our way to the courtroom to battle it out, when out of the blue, the infamous tapes emerged. Man Oh man, they were up the creek without a paddle when those tapes hit the airwaves. That is why we didn't need those so-called black leaders to come marching up to Texaco like somebody did them some type of injustice. They didn't go through a damn thing. When we needed them to get involved they weren't no place to be found. Just for the record, I know it should be (anywhere to be found) for all you grammar fanatics. I Need you all to realize that I am as highly educated as I say I am. But let me tell you the story about how the tapes emerged. It really goes back to that level of arrogance that had saturated this organization. You see, Texaco was downsizing and as fate would have it, one of the Executives that got caught in the net of the downsizing happened to record all the secret meetings, because he was the secretary and used to record the meetings so he could later do the minutes. So when he was threatened with losing his job, he threatened Texaco that he had something and if they fired him, they would be sorry. Of course you know we don't deal with terrorist threats, so basically they told him they could care less, and let him go. Thus the tapes surfaced on the lead plaintiffs desk. I had a lady friend in Texaco who once told me Texaco screws everyone. Don't take it personal. It's just that they screw us even more. I began to realize that it was true after the event with the tapes and how they emerged. Texaco really thought that they were God. You do have to realize that there were powerful people in powerful positions in Texaco, especially at the World Headquarters. They had lavish offices and people would jump at their command, just like they were Caesar or a Pharaoh in Egypt. You have to admit that is serious. Hell, I couldn't wait until it was my turn to be on the so-called Mahogany Row, where all the senior level executives played. But as we are still finding out today, "the good-ole boys" ain't having it. So there they were in these meetings calling us *niggas, porch monkeys,* and all types of derogatory names. For all you *House Negroes* who think you are exempt, think again jackasses. They were talking about you too. Sure, Texaco emphatically, and categorically denied that the tapes said *niggas*, and hired their own voice specialist who went on ABC's Nightline to defend that the tapes didn't say *niggas*, but in fact they said something about Saint Nicholas. You know it is amazing, just as amazing as the Rodney King videotapes. There they were beating the '*shit*' out of Rodney King and somehow they convinced a jury that that wasn't what happened. Hey, you pathetic *House Negroes*, remember that! I remember the CEO of Texaco on BET. For those of you who may not know what BET stands for, it is Black Entertainment Television. You could see the steam coming out of his head and ears. You could feel the humiliation he was going through having to sit there on this Black Television station and try to explain what happened, but let me tell you about those pathetic *House Negroes*. As Texaco, in its bid to try and save face, went after a few of the Executives that were identified on the tapes, who had recently retired from the company anyway, and then threatened the gentleman's pension who surrendered the tapes, those *House Negroes* wanted to take part of the money that we were receiving from the settlement to help him with his legal fees since he had taken ill and couldn't afford his attorney. I guess one could say how humane of those individuals. But what they didn't realize is that he was one of the main culprits on the tapes, laughing and calling us black jellybeans. See, there is a fundamental difference between the *House Negro* and the *Field Negro*. The *House Negro* says, "*massa* we sick?" while the *Field Negro* says, "hope your ass dies and rot in hell for raping and beating my mother, and sister, and for killing my father." I guess that is why it is so important that we had to adopt Christianity as our way of life. We had to be taught that to forgive is divine, and turn the other cheek was the right way to live. Isn't it funny though, how the slave masters who forced this upon us didn't practice any of it them self? Hell, they would beat a slave to death in a minute and lynch him in half the time. I venture to guess that if you didn't act like a good *House Negro,* then I guess you would probably end up a dead *Field Negro.* I also venture to guess that they got so good at acting like one that they forgot that they were acting. Some may say we've come a mighty long way from the days of the plantation as a people and a nation, however, the disparities, especially economically, still loom larger than ever between whites and blacks. So why is that? We are not less educated. We are not less qualified. Yet we still lag far behind. However, we do still remain the majority in the prisons of this country. Liberty and justice for all is not the theme practiced in the Courtrooms of America, and even though we won the lawsuit, prior to the emergence of those tapes, we were going to be in for the fight of our lives. Maybe if we would have went to court some of our so-called black leaders would have made a statement on our behalf. You know what, Texaco would have had a great defense in court if we wouldn't have won by default, because out of the one hundred or so black employees that were at Corporate Headquarters, where there were well over two thousand employees, only five of us gave depositions. All they would have had to say is, if we were treating our slaves, I mean employees so badly, then how come there are only five employees complaining? Good question. Yet conversely, those same employees, I mean slaves, the ones who made sure they stayed as far from the five of us during the lawsuit, were the first ones calling to find out when we were going to get the money from the settlement. Bastards! Can you believe that? *Pathetic ass motha fuckas*! Maybe now you can begin to see why there are certain things about them that really piss me off. I swear and I hate swearing, but these useless *niggas* get on my damn nerves. I've been trying to keep it clean, but I have got to keep it real. They are garbage. You know when people used to tell me I should write a book about Texaco, I would say yeah maybe, but what they didn't know was that I was always contemplating writing a book about those pathetic *House Negro*es at Texaco. Let me tell you something else about these people. The ones who had been there the longest, all of a sudden became real brave and remembered how to speak. They had the nerve to state that they should get the most money because they had suffered the longest. When the lawyers told me this, I nearly blew my top. Those cowards, and I'm being kind because I really want to call them the scum of the earth that they really are. I was so totally disgusted with them, you can't even begin to imagine. There they were, "We won, we won, God is good." I'm like, we who? But you know what? The real war was just about to begin, and those pitiful *House Negro*es were about to catch it like Mississippi Burning and they didn't have a clue, because they were thinking that they were accepted, and since they didn't actively seek action against Texaco they were also thinking there wouldn't be any repercussions. I almost feel sorry for them. I do, however, need to make one thing clear for the record about Texaco before I go on. At the Corporate World

Headquarters of Texaco, it wasn't like Texaco was this monster or insensitive company that had no regard for its Black employees. The only problem arose when it came time to promoting us based on our professional and educational credentials. We all got along well. I mean with the Whites. Probably because they were in charge and knew we would never be a threat of being their superior. But personally, I really loved Texaco. When I bought my first car, brand new may I add, all I used to buy was Texaco gas, and when I would change my oil, all I would use was Texaco oil. It was like we were married. I was loyal to Texaco. But once I felt betrayed, well, we all know how divorce can be and usually is ugly, well things just got real ugly. True, Texaco gave me a job, and at the time, the best job I ever had, but I had a dream deeply rooted in the American dream. What one must realize is that there is a big difference between having a career and having a job. There were times when you would hear things like, be glad you have a job. But in an organization such as Texaco one should rightfully expect nothing less than a career. I remember my older cousin who was a career Navy man said to me when I was visiting him out in California after I graduated from college, "You don't believe in that American Dream nonsense?" Shocked, I didn't know what to say, but when I thought about it, I realized that I really did and still do. However, when I say the Pledge of Allegiance to the flag I can't help but feel that liberty and justice is not being given to my people. I can't understand why, because of the color of our skin, we still have to fight this battle. I blame part of this on the ineffective leadership that has been thrust upon us ever since they systematically took out Malcolm and Martin. I mean, how is it in the year 2007 we have to be re-certified to be able to vote? Who else has to do that bullshit? Nothing personal, but I wonder what people like Oprah would do if the Republicans decided to mount an attack to stop the Voting Rights Act from being re-certified just to pay the Democrats back for threatening to filibuster, just enough to disrupt the 2008 presidential election. Imagine that! Boy oh boy, Blacks would be running around screaming bloody murder, and marching all over the place, yet half don't even vote still to this day. The so-called black leaders would be in front of the cameras screaming this is a travesty, and the Republicans are a bunch of racists, but they are the reason we are in these types of compromising situations in the 21st century. I wonder if they would let Oprah vote? Technically, she is Black, even though she is Republican. I wonder if you could be exempt if you are a Black Republican? One thing for sure, it wouldn't matter, because without the Black vote Democrats don't stand a chance. Then why is it that we continue to let them take our vote for granted? I'll tell you why. It's those puppets endorsing these Democrats for their own personal gain, just like when they came marching up to Texaco. Trust me, they did not leave empty handed. So are we going to continue to be granted permission to vote again the next time our Voting Rights come up for renewal? I guess we probably will. Hell, Johnson didn't want to pass the Voting Rights Act when he did. King demanded it. Realize that this was in the sixties when this fight to vote was taking place. They thought that after giving us Civil Rights that was good enough. I'm sure glad King knew better. And I'm really glad that he made things happen before this next batch of so-called leaders came along. You know we are always ready to blame Whites for the quagmire we are in, but we need to start holding those who think they are representing us accountable also. Look how long the Black people who worked at Texaco sat there and never said one word. There were some people who were there for over twenty years. So whose fault is it? Really, when you stop to think about it, if those spineless *House Negro*es would have spoken up years before, it is quite possible that Texaco could have been a place for me to have a career. If they would have been as quick to speak up when the CEO settled and were demanding that they should get the most money because of seniority, versus sitting quietly while being abused by this systemic racial culture festering inside this organization, Texaco could have probably been an ideal company to work for. My point is that those who sit and say nothing are just as responsible for the problems. Until we realize that we have a responsibility for our destiny we aren't going to be worth much of anything to anybody. There is a very interesting variable that is necessary to highlight because it's the truth about the who, how, and why these things and these individuals sat around and never said a damn thing. When you take a real in- depth look into Texaco's hiring practices pertaining to Blacks, you will find that most of the Blacks hired by Texaco were not born in this Country. Out of the one hundred or so of us that were there, maybe only ten were actually born in the USA. So what's my point? Maybe they didn't give a damn about the American Dream and maybe this was the best thing that ever happened to them. Who really knows except for them. And maybe fear kept them silent. The other truth is that before this lawsuit many of the people from the Islands put their race as 'other' versus Black on their employment application. But when the lawsuit was being settled and it was determined it was only for those individuals in the database listed as Black as their race, boy oh boy did they scream loud and hard that they were Black. Also, there was only one individual from the Islands who was part of the lawsuit. So I guess you must be wondering where were the rest of them who just discovered they had been abused the longest. Well your guess is as good as mine. If it were up to me, they would have been totally excluded from receiving any monetary award. They damn sure didn't deserve to be included. I have no respect for them, and if you can't understand why, well I don't know what to say. It seems pretty damn obvious. You know I used to always hear so much about Marcus Garvey from the people from the Islands and how he, along with so many of them, stood up and fought against the white man. I just can't figure out what happened here. I guess it is what it is. At least this wasn't classed as some minority lawsuit. It was by Blacks for Blacks. Sort of like that FUBU, for us by us. But by the time those sell-outs got finished with their input about the settlement, which I will talk about later, Texaco was saying it was going to look at all minorities, which automatically meant that Blacks were not going to be the primary beneficiary of this lawsuit. So guess who became the primary beneficiary? White women. I never saw so many White women promoted in Texaco in all my ten years. You knew, because they were all of a sudden sporting three and sometimes four window offices. Remember, that was how you could tell one's status in Texaco, by the amount of windows they had. If you had a corner office you had six windows. That was usually reserved for the head of the department. Get the picture! And there weren't any Blacks with a corner office anywhere in Corporate Headquarters, before, during or after the lawsuit, and none with four window offices. Maybe one with a three window, the EEOC who Texaco paraded around like a guinea pig during the lawsuit. It's interesting how we were the majority of minorities in Texaco and probably benefited the least after the lawsuit. The few Hispanics that were employed at Texaco felt wronged, but they never said anything either until after we won and received that record 175 million dollar settlement. It's like winning the lottery and all of a sudden all your long lost relatives come out of nowhere expecting a hand out. We continually are in the forefront of movements for justice and equality and bearing the brunt of the retaliation, but continue to benefit the least, and this has got to stop. We have got to stop letting people use us, and stop our leaders from using us, while we continue to reap nothing from it. The Democrats only come around when they need our support via our leaders, yet, when we need them, where are they?

They become as invisible as the Black leaders who brought them to our neighborhoods. Yet we continue to support them. The other alternative, the Republicans are still even a worse alternative for us, even if the Hispanics have appeared to find solace with them. Good for them and I wish them well, but we have got to find a solution to this dilemma plaguing us, and I think we need to do this by re-examining the people who say they represent us. We need to let them know that they don't represent a damn thing, but themselves. Next time they come to one of our neighborhoods we ought to run them the hell out. You may wonder why I am on this so strongly. Well, I'll tell you this, I don't know who the hell negotiated the settlement, but by the time it was over the Class was screwed royally. These individuals who were supposed to be our representatives, so to speak, sold us right out. Whatever they negotiated for themselves we will never really know, but after they went away, and the lawsuit was decided, and made public, you will see why this whole thing was a fiasco. When you really stop to think about it, tell me, can you think of anything worthwhile that has manifested from anything our so-called black leaders have done in the past ten or even fifteen years? If so, please tell me because I surely would like to know. Take a really good look at the NAACP and the Rainbow Coalition. They are a joke, and nobody respects them. NAACP is still walking around calling themselves colored people. I mean really!

Chapter 4

The Settlement

After all was said and done, everyone who was directly involved with this lawsuit was pissed off, considering all we had to endure to get to this point. The lawyers were pissed because they didn't get the lump sum they wanted. The lead plaintiffs who gave depositions didn't get any substantial award for the risk taken in bringing forth this action against Texaco, and for that fact, neither did anyone who gave depositions against Texaco. So the only ones who benefited were the ones who got the free ride. That also includes the ones who came marching up to Texaco with their hand out. Trust me, the Rainbow Coalition got paid. I remember reading an article in the Wall Street Journal about the formula used to determine who got what, and even they were perplexed by the distribution of this award. They said something like a CPA couldn't even figure this out, or Ph.D for that matter. The other critical factor that went under the radar was that the monies were awarded as wages. So what does that mean? It means that everything was taxable, that's what that means. Not only was everything taxable, it put everyone in the highest tax bracket. They held back millions for payroll, FICA, unemployment, and whatever else you could imagine, and the list goes on. Oh yeah, there was a Special Task Force formed which was for the sole purpose of monitoring Texaco and it's practices of hiring and handling any complaints or concerns from the Class, and compliance with the Court Order. Sounds good, right? There were three people from the plaintiffs side and three representing Texaco's interest with a Chairperson. All this was going to cost was $35,000,000.00. Imagine that! Who the hell made this garbage up, thirty five million, for what? The lawyers received about twenty million on some type of sliding scale on a per year basis, but it was a far cry from the lump sum they were looking for. I personally think lawyers benefit the most from these types of lawsuits, but this time I understood their displeasure. After that they weren't even taking our calls anymore. No idea of how many millions were held for those other taxes but you can best believe it was several million. Mind you, it took about a year or so before the first dollar was ever distributed. Truly it was a fiasco. I remember getting calls daily from you know who, those useless, pathetic, worthless individuals, about when were we going to get paid. The lawyers even opened up an 800 number for anyone from the Class to call regarding any concerns about the money, addresses, etc. But every time there was a call there was a charge. You would think after all the taxes that were held, our tax obligations would have been satisfied. Hell, our tax obligations were just beginning. I do see why when you have money you want to be Republican because those taxes are a monster if you don't have places you can hide or write off that income. Well after the legal parameters were established, Texaco was ready to go back to business as usual. But they really didn't have to because there was such a backlash from the white employees, even

Texaco was not prepared to handle. First the lead plaintiffs were systematically removed from the Corporate Headquarters. One was on special assignment to his church and the woman went on to write a book about Texaco. You know what's interesting? She was there maybe five years before she pursued this action. It makes me wonder if there is a fundamental difference between how we as African Americans feel about the equality issue versus how our brothers and sisters from the Islands feel about it? I am still trying to figure out how and why would someone sit in a position knowingly, now obviously knowing (since they wanted the most money for being there the longest and suffering the most) that they are being mistreated professionally. Anyway, it's only the three of us left who had given depositions against the company. They systematically removed the two lead plaintiffs out of the company so there wouldn't be any more trouble. This actually would allow Texaco and the Task Force to do what they wanted, with them out of the way. There were no checks and balances in the system with them out of the way. No follow up by the news of how things were progressing and if there was any retaliation afterwards, things like that. Texaco would have remained in the spotlight for a while if they were still employees at Headquarters. However, Texaco quickly took care of that. The others weren't a threat before and weren't about to become one now. The white people who used to speak to me were no longer saying hello. You know what's really interesting, was that before the CEO settled, the whites were apologizing about the racist comments on the tapes. After we got paid they were mad as hell. Make no mistake about it, they were not hiding their displeasure even with the CEO for settling. They wanted to get rid of him too. Does it threaten white people that much if we have money? Apparently it does. I guess that is why there continues to be this tremendous disparity of income for us compared to them. So if this is true and I have come to believe that it is, you can begin to imagine what the atmosphere was like in the halls of the Corporate Headquarters in White Plains, N.Y., however, I'm not sure what the hell was going on in Houston, Texas. I had a friend in Texas who worked at the office in downtown Houston who used to tell me stories about how it was down there and I couldn't believe my ears. However, after going to school in Florida it sounded pretty accurate to me. She even told me of a white women's club they had in the Houston office. Who knows, maybe they did, but who really cares? I don't. Nothing really mattered at this time because Texaco was in control of everything anyway. Now that everything was going to be based on minorities, this was allowing Texaco to manipulate its required reporting to the Court. No one ever asked the question, what percentage were African Americans in those numbers. No one really cared. Now here was a real opportunity for those who supposedly claimed to represent us to ask these types of questions, but where were they? Once again we had been hoodwinked, duped, used and manipulated with no recourse. After the cameras were gone so were they. There was never any kind of follow-up, like Texaco a year later, after the lawsuit. Nothing!

Absolutely nothing. One reason was because Texaco had promised to do more business within the Black community. And after a few organizations received a few dollars, it was like putting a pacifier in a baby's mouth. You know those *House Negro*es. They kick and scream for a little while, then nothing. Throw them a bone and they shut up, just like a little puppy. The first year, Texaco supported the Universal Soul Circus, the only African American circus in America. After the second year, that was over. Just to give you an idea of how they were doing business. So the new Texaco looked like this. A few well educated individuals got a cramped two window office, and a couple of promotions went to those who kept their mouth shut during the lawsuit and the rest were a onslaught of white women who were placed into middle management. All that mattered was that the numbers reflected what was required by the Court, and that's just what Texaco was doing, meeting the requirements. So what was this Task Force suppose to be doing for $35,000,000.00? Well, the Chair who was an African American was the one who was to monitor Texaco. Everyone again was raving about how this individual was so great. It always scares me when they say someone is such a great person. I reminded my fellow colleague that he said the same thing about the EEOC. Anyway I saw him one day in the cafeteria, but I choose not to introduce myself. But my colleague was so gung ho about this Chairperson, so I let him do his thing. I just sat on the sidelines and watched. There were a few other people who were very impressed with him and asked me had I met him. I simply replied no.

One reason why I chose not to was because he was too buddy, buddy with the former EEOC. The EEOC was the individual who Texaco used to defend their position during the lawsuit. It's interesting the things one may do even if he knows he is dead wrong. But I guess he didn't have much of a choice. Maybe he should have thought about not taking that position before they offered it to him, as he had suggested to me. At least I could sleep at night in good conscience. You know, because of his position he probably got a higher award than most of us, since it was based on your salary compared to the white employees of the company. Even at his position, he was only in the teens as far as his grade level. Since he was against us in this lawsuit you might think that he would recuse himself from receiving that money. Ain't no way that was happening. I guess you have to admit, it pays to be a good *House Negro*. It sure did for him and all the rest of them who sat and watched. What a fiasco. But that ain't all. To make things look even better, the CEO immediately recruited this life long African American employee of Texaco out of the Houston Headquarters to be the liaison to all the Black people who were begging Texaco for funds, since Texaco had said it was going to do a substantial amount of business within the Black Business Community. Now you would think that that would be a good thing, but I don't know of many who benefited from this, especially since I became part of the NY/NJ Minority Purchasing Council. Texaco was dangling a carrot in front of all these vendors who were hoping to get just one contract with Texaco. I watched while they used various

Minorities to set up stations for vendors to leave their card and information for Texaco to contact them. Like I said, I know the Circus got some money for a year, maybe even two, but that was it. So much for the liaison they recruited. But the African American community was so thrilled about this appointment when it hit the headlines in the papers. Texaco hires African American as Special Assistant to CEO. It wasn't like he was advising the CEO on how the company should proceed, or as if he was in the Board meetings with the other senior level executives. He was a showpiece, a pacifier, and decoy, to silence the critics about Texaco. Guess what? It worked. They were praising the CEO about his commitment to making Texaco a better work environment for minorities. They didn't have a clue about what was really going on. That is why it really was necessary for the lead plaintiffs to remain on the scene after the lawsuit at least for a year. It would have at least kept things honest. They should have been appointing them to some real position in the company. That would have been a true test to monitor how serious Texaco was. Once they sent one on special assignment to his church and basically gave the other the ultimatum, can't write your book and stay here, they knew she was going to leave. These were the lead plaintiffs. They were privy to information me and my other colleague didn't have. So basically we were left hung out to dry. Yeah we got some money, but remember we were now receiving 1099 reporting forms from the IRS. I had never seen one of them before in my life even though I knew what it was. I knew enough not to play around with them. I do remember sending in $20,000 dollars when I first received that 1099. The attorney's told us we should pay a certain percentage just to be on the safe side. I did just that, however many people didn't. You know our M-O, we buy cars first and fancy jewelry, and nothing of redeemable value. We do what we do best. Consume. As far as I was concerned, that money didn't mean a damn thing. We needed to be concerned about our future with this company. Since we didn't have the lead plaintiffs anymore, my colleague and I tried to keep the Class abreast since we did still have some communication with the attorney's from the New York office. I spoke to some of the Class at one of our Black History Month Committee meetings, that if there were any problems they should utilize the Task Force. Hell, the Task Force was getting $35,000,000.00. Make them earn some of that money. I still wonder who decided to give them thirty five million dollars. We could have certainly used that money. Hell, those who gave depositions should have gotten that money. I think they sat down and figured out how not to give this money to us *niggas*, I mean Black Folks. So the important *House Negro*es were so happy about Texaco and its progress because of one appointment. It's a damn shame that they can be so easily pacified. That is why I said I am so glad King fought on after the Civil Rights to get the Voting Rights Act. It is that mentality of those *House Negro*es, who are so easily pacified, that they would probably have been satisfied with just Civil Rights and we probably wouldn't have been able to vote for another twenty-five years. It's scary. That is why I talk more about the damage these *House Negro*es have caused and are still causing till this day. They settle, or are so easily pacified, that they are a real danger to our future. I mean, just because the position sounded good, there should have been some real questions asked by our leaders who were so appalled by the racist remarks caught on the tapes. They should have been asking, so is this a senior level position. Is he going to be involved in the hiring process of minorities, especially African Americans? What exactly will he be doing? If they would have took the time out to find that out, they would have also found out that the position was bogus. One day I went to speak with him upon recommendation of my Coach, who I will discuss later, and to be honest, I was like "do I have to?" I was so sick of talking to people who couldn't do much if anything for me, but I did it anyway. We actually had an interesting conversation, and he shared some things with me that proved to be pretty interesting. I knew that he didn't want the position as liaison for all those Black vendors seeking money from Texaco, because his desire was to run one of the operational departments. Made sense to me, only thing I couldn't figure out was that after thirty years with the company how come he hadn't had the opportunity to do so by now? Personally, he should have been the lead plaintiff in this lawsuit. I mean after thirty years with a company you should be somewhere in the running, or on the short list for CEO, yet alone running operations. Being at the Corporate World Headquarters allowed me to be privy to certain things, and one of them was knowing that they were never going to let a Black run any Operations. So when he shared that he wanted to run one of the operational departments, I just smiled and thought to myself you must be out of your damn mind. I do know that given his thirty plus years with Texaco he made out like a bandit from the settlement, even though he had nothing and probably didn't want anything to do with it. I'm sure he didn't. Hell, I guess by now you know how I feel about that. After that meeting I began to realize one thing, and that was, Texaco will give you some money, but they ain't gonna give you no real position within the Organization. Just ain't happening. That's how I know they paid off the leaders of those organizations, because you didn't hear one word from them afterwards. And you wonder why I have such contempt for them. I remember one day while I was in the gym with my workout buddy and we were discussing the events at Texaco, he said, to my surprise, we need to purge our race of those damn *House Negro*es. I was like, "damn baby-boy where did that come from." This was a well-read individual, highly intelligent brother. He started telling me how the KKK don't deal with those idiots wearing hoods anymore. They recruit from the best schools and make sure that their people get in those key positions in Corporate America, like the ones in Texaco that you can't and never will get into. That's how they control things. Very interesting wouldn't you say. As he continued, he said those *House Negro*es are like a cancer. So I asked what should we do with them? What can we really do with them legally? Nothing! I guess we are stuck with them. That really concerns me regarding the future of my people. When you stop and look around right now in the 21st century, we are struggling as much as we were in the sixties, before the Civil Rights movement. Your boy Ronnie saw to the total unraveling of the movement, but then again, how much unraveling could he really do if the Democrats were really for us. Remember when I mentioned Jesse ran for the presidency, and he did extremely well I might add. He even had enough delegates to force a primary. Instead, he settled for a speech at the Democratic Convention, preaching party unity, and keep hope alive. I wonder if he knew that we were getting ready to catch pure hell under this Republican Regime. He had to know. He received thunderous applause for his speech, you know, said a couple of rhymes and '*thangs*'. Then that was the end. The Democrats came up with that bogus platform of Dukakis and Lloyd Bentsen from Texas as the ticket against Regan/Bush?   Bentsen didn't even rate as a presidential candidate, and everyone with any political sense had to know that ticket couldn't win a damn thing. But the thought of potentially having a Black as Vice President of the United States must have scared them more than anything the Republicans might do. So did Regan really unravel the Civil Rights Movement? Or did the Democrats sacrifice us like the Romans used to sacrifice the Christians to the lions? Just like the thought of having a Black heading up Operations at Texaco was unheard of. I remember when a few of the fellows were hanging out after work, and my buddy who I used to work with delivering boxes at Texaco asked this white boy who worked in the mail room, what would he do if I became Supervisor of the Mailroom? He answered without any hesitation and said straight out he would quit. Imagine that. Me and this white boy, graduated from the same High School the same year. Now mind you, all he had was a high school diploma, and rather than work under me, he would rather quit working at Texaco. I'll tell you, I couldn't believe my ears, but then again I could. It was that type of mentality that has saturated most whites. They think they are superior to us and it doesn't matter if they ain't got pass elementary school, they feel they are still better than a *nigga*, I mean Blacks. But you do know that is what they call us. Right?

I guess they know that one day they are gonna reap what they have sown, so if I was them I guess I would be scared too, considering all the barbaric, and violent acts that they have perpetrated on us as a race. And since they know that money can open avenues, they spend all of their time making sure we don't acquire any wealth. They make sure we can't live in their neighborhoods. Yeah maybe one or two, but trust me, they watch very carefully. This country is still divided along racial parameters. We are the only ones going around preaching diversity. Take a good look at who runs the major firms on Wall Street. Take a good look at who is running Washington D.C. We ain't nowhere to be found in either of those arenas. That's where all the decisions are made. Why aren't we found anywhere if we are supposed to be such a diversified nation? What happened to 'keep hope alive'? I'll tell you what happened! Great speech! Boy, that is one articulate *nigga*. Wish I could get up there and rhyme like that there good old colored boy. Yeah he's a good one, stepped aside for the good of the Party. We need more like him. Remember when he was with King and used to wear that there, what them Africans call them things, oh yeah, Daishekis. Yeah that's it. Walked around with his hand raised doing that black power sign. Yeah he's really one of us now. I know you are probably saying they don't talk like that, but they got a bunch of tapes from Texaco that say all kinds of things about us, and these ain't some hillbillies from Mississippi, even though they don't feel any different about us than them hillbillies from Mississippi. These were top senior level executives of a major U.S. corporation. They were in their natural element. It was apparent that they spoke like this all the time. You better wake up before it's too late. I venture to think that it may already be. So Jesse went from damn near being a presidential nominee to what? Hell, makes me wonder what he was doing before the Texaco tapes? It wasn't like Texaco was the first and only company that was racist in their hiring and promotion of Blacks. I will say that Texaco was probably the worst considering most Corporations had at least a few tokens in decision-making positions within the organization, but Texaco had zero. That's right, zero. If you think I'm lying, go check. Ask anyone. There was not one Black in the entire company that was in Middle or Senior level Management. Sad but true. But again I'm faced with this dilemma, of who's fault was it really? I mean, if you are satisfied with picking cotton and getting a paycheck then what? Hell, if that's all you want I can't make you drink the water, and I damn sure ain't gonna just give it to you. So if that's all you want is to pick cotton, I guess that's all well and good, but I'll be damned if you are going to look down on me because you make a little more money than I do picking cotton, to make yourself feel like you're somebody when all you are is a passive, docile, contemporary slave. You know people who look down upon other people to make themselves feel better usually come with an inferiority complex. Psychology 101. You know what really angers me and scares me? These are the same type of people who would have never left Egypt or the plantation, even after Moses, even after the Emancipation Proclamation, even though that document was about as valuable as toilet tissue after you use it. Imagine, I could still be a slave if it was left up to these cowards. I don't know about the rest of you Black people, but it certainly scares the hell out of me that I could possibly, even if remotely, still be a slave because of these cowardly Negroes who would settle for picking cotton and have seniority picking cotton and be satisfied still picking cotton in the 21st century, as long as they got a paycheck every week. Extreme analogy, call it what you want, but it ain't far from the truth! Those *House Negro*es are a danger to us, and the American way of life. Every other group that has come over here knew they would have to work hard in order to get ahead. But getting ahead was always part of the equation. With the *House Negro* that philosophy does not exist. As long as he gets more crumbs that fall on the floor from the masters table than his brother that is in the field, he thinks he is doing good. And people wonder why Blacks are still in the quagmire they are in even at this point and time in history. Sure there were unconscionable ills placed upon us by our captors, but it surely wasn't any thanks to those *House Negro*es, how we overcame. Take a look at slavery from the point in time before America. There was a lucrative business going on with the Portuguese, who were the biggest slave traders ever. But when you look at slavery you must first look at the fact that it was a business, and we were traded by our own leaders. Sold for things as worthless as shaving bowls, can you believe it? What idiots! We need to think twice about who is responsible for our situation. We have to be held accountable for some of these evils we have placed and continue to place upon ourselves. For instance, in Texaco, Blacks had twenty, thirty years of employment in that organization, how could it be possible to not have anyone in Senior Management? How? Oh yeah the glass ceiling, right! Bullshit! Complacent, docile, pathetic *House Negro*es, that's all it was. Are you beginning to somewhat understand the detriment that these people cause? The irreparable damage! Sure Texaco is not without fault, make no mistake about that, however, it wasn't by any means entirely all their fault. Those *House Negro*es who sat around all during the lawsuit until they thought it was allegedly safe to claim their stake, then here they come crying I'm Black, and I'm entitled to more than you because I have seniority. Will somebody please shoot these biologically useless creatures. Please! Please! Please! They are a menace not only to us, but, to society. They are cancer, toxic waste.

One may wonder why I feel the way I do, so let me give an example of how detrimental they can be. I remember after causing all those problems with the memos I wrote to the Head of the department and they promoted me laterally to the Financial Planning Group in the Corporate Services Department. I was pissed about the lateral, but I had to perform. Eventually the Head of the Financial Planning Group assigned this Black female as my supervisor. Just supervising me, since I was the only other Black in the department, oh yeah there was one other. Just trying to be accurate. Since I was the troublemaker now, I guess it was up to her to straighten me out. This would make her look really good, since they couldn't do anything with me because I decided to go on the warpath. You know, even though we were going through our differences, me and Texaco, I always did my work and received good evaluations. They would say 'Pete you do great work', always. So here she comes my Black female supervisor with this evaluation that was basically the worst I ever had. "Here, look it over and return it to me." I was like "Okay." A few days passed by and she asked if I had signed it yet. "No not yet." I had a real serious decision to make. Now if I attack her, my Black sister, would that be wrong? Or if I didn't, this evaluation would go into my file and I would never get an interview in any department after that. This is how serious it was. Mind you, the lawsuit was still going on at this point in time. So if I let this evaluation go into my file and it was by a Black supervisor, and negative, I was dead. My question is why did she even try it? But she was one of those who had been with the company for over twenty years and was basically a bean counter, as they were often referred to in the department. Here was her big chance to show *massa* that she was a good overseer. She picked the wrong *nigga* to mess with. I chewed her up and spit her out, and spit out the manager of the Financial Planning Group while I was at it. I basically stated that she wasn't qualified to evaluate me. I said that without higher formal educational learning, there wasn't anyway that she or the Manager of the Group could be qualified to evaluate me. What is challenging to them is nothing but a mere task for me. So they keep giving me tasks that they feel are challenges, and for them they probably are challenges. Man I felt so bad when I returned my evaluation in to her, but it had to be done. After that, I was called upstairs by my Manager's boss, and he changed the evaluation. You know they were pissed with me from that point forward. I'll tell you this, if I was some good ole *House Negro* I would have sat there and accepted it. On the other hand, if I was some good ole *House Negro* I probably would have gotten a satisfactory review in the first place, got my increase and that would have been enough crumbs off of the masters table. Personally, I don't give a damn about none of it as long as you respect me. You can pay me garbage wages, you can promote me laterally and whatever else, but if you dare disrespect me, or insult my intelligence, your behind is mine, as many found out in Texaco. You may say paying me garbage wages is disrespectful and an insult to my intelligence, and you are right, but don't think I am out in the field saying *massa* ain't so bad. Trust me, I'm gonna get you. Remember one thing, I was always in the gym everyday bench pressing 300lbs., running 5 miles everyday at lunchtime, so pick your poison. You can only push me so far, trust me. They should be glad I was educated, cause someone might have gotten seriously hurt. They should be thankful I learned the pen is mightier than the sword, as my memos to the CEO were becoming the talk of Texaco. After being with the company nearly nine years at this point in time, I basically had zero tolerance for any of their nonsense. Anything I had to say was going directly to the CEO. I was through talking to those figureheads that couldn't do a damn thing, or wouldn't do a damn thing for me. It had gotten to the point that my last memo to the CEO read something to the effect, I know you are about as tired of hearing from me as I am of writing to you, however, and boy oh boy, the power of the pen. You see, after the tapes were exposed the CEO was adamant that there would be zero tolerance for any racism or discrimination and there would be zero tolerance for any type of retaliation. So I was daring anyone to challenge that position. But just because he said it, didn't mean that there wasn't going to be any. So every concern I had, I made it my personal business to include him even sometimes as bcc. That's blind cover copy so they wouldn't know I sent it to him. Personally, I was having fun with them. I was enjoying terrorizing them with my memos. They feared the pen, and I wasn't hesitating to use it. It was like being a slave master with a whip, and I whipped them every chance I got. I used to wake up in the middle of the night, just like I am doing right now, and write. I will share the incident that brought me into the spotlight and the memo that was written by me that almost brought Texaco to its knees begging the Newspaper not to print that story. Now instead of walking around clean-shaven looking like a company man, I was sporting my full-grown beard and walking around like I was straight up in the hood. The hood means the ghetto for you *House Negro*es who may not understand. I expect that there are some who may not understand some of the vernacular, and at times while I am composing this thesis I do revert to ghetto street language, but I will try to bridge the gap, as I want all who read this to understand what exactly is being presented. I also hope that you may be able to identify those *House Negro*es and eventually weed them out for yourself, for all of our sakes. Even though I had become a real thorn, I had made it my personal business to never be late and actually had perfect attendance two years in a row. I was going to make it real difficult for the enemy. The enemy, yeah, it was us against them but it is still us against these *House Negro*es. You know, even though I majored in Management and Economics I also minored in Sociology and Psychology. I mention this because I have a tendency to critique how different groups and cultures interact with each other, versus the way we as Blacks, and those who consider themselves "Other", interact with each other. For example, when I am in the gym I watch how the Hispanics interface with each other and I have found that even though they may do menial labor, like mopping the floors, cleaning the locker room, the equipment, the mirrors, whatever, I have never seen their women, or fellow brethren greet them any less than with decency and respect. It's always hola, como sta, bien! Don't get me wrong, I know that there are some real legitimate issues within their culture, however, they are making tremendous strides collectively. During the World Series or one of the Championship Divisional games, one of the owners was Hispanic. I thought to myself, that's very interesting. He owns a team and we are still trying to get them to let us be a coach of a team. Big difference. My point really is that they don't think any less of each other based on the type of jobs they may have. I will never forget, not only in Texaco, but all during my years of underemployment, how it was. Black women couldn't care less that I was educated. All it ever was, was where do you work, what kind of work do you do? They are too good to speak to a janitor. Somewhere, I guess being the best at whatever you are doing got tossed out the window. It is a shame that Malcolm and Martin were executed and make no mistake, I realize why. However, did we not learn anything from their sacrifices? I remember all too clearly being shunned by my fellow brethren and my sisters at Texaco. I felt like I was a leper or something. Okay that's a little exaggerated, because I always stayed well dressed in there. I used to laugh at them because while they used to try to ignore me, especially when they were in the company of whites and maybe an executive from Mahogany Row, and the executive would say 'hey Pete How are you, go running today'? You should have seen the look on their faces. It's pitiful, a crying shame that we feel we have to treat each other with less than respect because we are afraid that if the whites think we associate with someone in a lesser position than oneself it will have a negative outcome for that individual. Maybe they don't realize or are not aware of what they are doing. If they are aware of it then maybe my gym partner is right about the fact we need to purge our race of these toxic, poisonous Negroes.

Shortly after our Class Action Lawsuit, there was a Lawsuit filed by the professional women of Texaco. This lawsuit got settled quickly, before the media had the chance to get a hold of it. The amount was undisclosed, however I knew a Black woman who fit the criteria for this lawsuit. The interesting part about their settlement was that it didn't have all the particulars ours had. It was plain and simple, damages, no taxes, no Task Force for $35,000,000.00, none of that. I ask myself why? All I can say is that whatever we are involved in we don't take control of it. We always let someone else dictate our outcome. That's why we are still trying to be coaches while others are trying to be owners. Those who supposedly are our representatives run around honoring this one for this and that one for that, but in actuality they haven't accomplished much of anything in a very long time that is for the good of all of the people. They are weak and pathetic and the purge should begin with them.

Chapter 5

The Aftermath

So here we are, the lead plaintiffs are now gone for whatever reasons, and are nothing more than an after thought, and even though the CEO is going around ensuring that there will be no retaliation and zero tolerance for racism, don't think for one moment that revenge was not on their minds. It was now about being smarter than before. Texaco was not about to become this kinder, gentler organization to work for, for minorities. Well at least not for Blacks and those who had recently discovered they were Black. What one must realize is that there were some very serious players at the Corporate Headquarters. The CEO used to rule with an Iron hand. As we would say in the streets, there was nothing soft about him. A lot of people feared him, even executives, but personally, I kind of admired his ruthless style. He would never smile, and would walk down the halls 'straight up, hard core'. I even heard he had eliminated a whole department at one time. I don't know if it was true, but no one messed with him. I remember one day when I was running the Conference Center, yeah, we had our own Conference Center built inside the building, along with our own auditorium, where we had some very prominent people perform. Anyway, I'll tell you about the performing scenario in a minute. I was running this brand new state-of-the-art Center, which was for Senior Level Executives only. That's what I'm saying, they put me in charge of it. Imagine that! I ran that Center flawlessly. So one day at the pre-board meeting where all the Department Heads of

Operating Divisions, (got together to discuss the strategy for the board meeting), were having a break, laughing outside in the lounge area, the CEO who was then a Senior VP came back from his office from the break, saw them in the lounge area and in this stern cutting voice said "Gentlemen"! Man they jumped like they saw Jesus Christ walking on water or something. I was like damn, that's serious. I tell you this because you need to understand the culture that existed inside Corporate Headquarters. It was a demanding environment, with no mistakes allowed. Everyone who wasn't on Mahogany Row, walked in fear. So if you think for one moment that there wasn't going to be hell to pay, you are sadly mistaken. Believe you me, there was about to be some lynching on this plantation. I'm telling you, this was no place for the weak and docile now. I guess, before, if you just sat there like a good ole *House Negro* you were safe, but just like when the White slave masters used to get mad at the Blacks during slavery, they would kill any and all. Men, women and children. I know you good ole *House Negro*es forgot all about those times, so it would be easier for you to be accepted and fit in. It's like if you renounce your blackness, your heritage, you're in. Well, since my childhood began at the time of integration, I feel compelled to share some of the things that I have learned from being integrated, that those sorry *House Negro*es may never learn. Back in the early sixties before busing really started, while in elementary school, full of white students, and 'Say it Loud I'm Black and I'm Proud', by James Brown was the latest hit song, I remember how those white kids used to snicker and laugh because I couldn't write in script in third grade. I also remember that my spelling was really good, however, my math skills were superior. I knew up to my twelve times table in second grade. So when it came time for writing in script, I hated it, but when it was time for spelling and math, I was the man. Soon the snickering stopped because I was also becoming proficient in script, but it stopped mainly because I was superior in mathematics. Probably has something to do with my African ancestry. My point is that I was proud of who I was and I wasn't about to be oppressed by their antics. I wasn't going to walk around like I was stupid just because I couldn't write very well in script. I had other attributes, even though at that time I didn't know what attributes meant. But I know I had them, and of course I was physically superior. Hell, I was stronger and faster than all of them. And what I found out was that they spent more time trying to beat me physically. So I automatically felt superior. As hard as they would try, they could never beat me in any sport. So *House Negro*, be proud of who you are. Don't compromise so easily just to be accepted. People died for us to be where we are today. I wonder sometimes, how far have we really come? Well that's another topic, however being subservient ain't doing us as a people any damn good. The funny thing is that there are a lot of Black people out there who really think they are representing. We have spent so much time trying to emulate them, while they have spent so much time emulating us, that they are better emulating us than we are ourselves. When you go to the gym, who do you see working out?

Blacks or Whites? Mostly Whites. Look who is in better shape now, Black women or White women? White women. There was a time when Black women were the most beautiful women around. Now it's hard to find one with her own hair. Black women became so preoccupied with being accepted, once they became this double minority and the preferred group for employment in Corporate America when Affirmative Action was alive, trying to emulate white women and date white men and who knows what else, that they lost everything. See, the white man knows that the Black woman is the backbone for us. Our women are so liberated now, that there ain't no Black man good enough for them. Look at who is having the most abortions. Us or them? I bet you we are. Well, if you think that trying to be like them is going to save you, let me tell you about the aftermath in Texaco following the lawsuit. The new corporate term 'right-sizing' was implemented like McDonalds uses 'super-size'. They began 'right-sizing' those Negroes right the hell up out of there, along with the new corporate term, 'the brightest and the best'. All those Negroes who were concerned about when they were going to get their money now had to be concerned about when they were going to find another job. They were dropping like flies in there. Now who was watching that? NAACP where you at? Rainbow Coalition, where you at? I'll tell you where they were! They were sucking on that pacifier that Texaco stuck in their mouth! Whole departments were being castrated. The only difference was that they were giving employees a chance to see if there were opportunities in other departments. So that way it wouldn't look like Blacks were being targeted. This also, subliminally allowed, those who were entirely disenfranchised about the whole settlement, to incorporate their friends. While Blacks were allowed to apply to different departments, I don't know of anyone who was caught in this massive right-sizing campaign, who got positions in another department. I remember someone saying to me that God is getting all of his people out of here. Maybe he was. I think that Texaco was getting rid of as many of us as it could without being cited. Sounds a bit more logical and accurate to me, knowing Texaco. You know, being fired is one thing, but then to be escorted out of the building is another. I was determined that I wasn't going out that way. Personally, I didn't feel sorry for those who were being led to the slaughter. Not everyone was deserving of that, but the majority were. It's interesting how White people want to talk to you when they become victimized. As long as it isn't them, they could care less. Once it's them, all of a sudden the CEO is a jerk, this company sucks, etc. Save it. By this time I was basically resigned to the fact, that the sooner someone takes this company over, the better. For the most part, those of us who gave depositions were more or less untouchable. I was so sick of hearing from different people how they should have said something and they should have joined the lawsuit. But as soon as Texaco threw them a bone they were happy as a pig in shit. I was hoping someone would really take this company over and throw all those sorry, pathetic *House Negro*es out, but most of the Blacks at Headquarters were already gone. If there were twenty of us after the right-sizing campaign, that would be stretching it. Soon the other plaintiff's assignment at his church was up and he wanted to come back to work at Corporate Headquarters. You know that wasn't happening, and he probably didn't want to come back either, but they got one of the House-boys to suggest to him an alternative. Actually, it was the former EEOC, it's amazing how we just keep selling each other out. Finally, they paid him to go away. I bet, if you trace the lineage of the EEOC back to Africa, he probably comes from one of those groups who sold their people into slavery. You may ask how could Texaco do all this and get away with it? I'll tell you how. They kept finding creative ways to make it look like they were progressively making strides in their hiring of African Americans. Promote a few old ones and hire a few new ones, and I mean a few. But the one with the most significance and the one that was the most unethical was about to happen. But those *House Negroes* were too busy praising Texaco to even realize the unethical nature surrounding the hiring of this individual. Fools!

Remember the Task Force I was telling you about that cost the Class thirty-five million dollars? Well the Chairman of the Task Force, the one responsible for monitoring Texaco's compliance and reporting back to the Court, was all of a sudden chosen to be General Counsel for Texaco approximately one year later. Yep! That's absolutely correct! The one responsible for reporting to the Courts about Texaco's progress is now head of the Legal Department at Texaco.

Now maybe I'm just stupid or something, but tell me, isn't there something the hell wrong with that picture? Obviously not, because every event that I would attend that were Black affairs, mostly those the executives didn't want to be bothered with, there they were inquiring about Texaco. They would say things like, 'isn't it great the progress they are making at Texaco'. They have a Black as Assistant to the CEO, the former EEOC heading a newly created position for African Americans and now, the Chair of the Diversity Task Force is General Counsel for Texaco. This was all bullshit and these stupid ass Negroes were praising Texaco like they were at Sunday Morning Worship. The first two positions, for whatever reason, I can live with, however, that whole General Counsel thing was too much for me to swallow. I mean, there were people who had confided in him, like my colleague who swore by the EEOC. I tell you, whenever someone tells me about how great someone is, and this and that, I always hold back before meeting them. This time I was really glad I did. After the report was in to the Courts, he became General Counsel. Now I would have had more respect if the report wasn't as favorable towards Texaco, but then you know they would have never made him General Counsel. So right there, there is a conflict of interest. I just felt that it was unethical. I recently came across an article where the former Chair of the Task Force was explaining the chain of events that transpired when approached about the position of General Counsel for Texaco. He said the Judge gave him approval to have these talks with Texaco. He also said he felt that he could do more good on the inside per se. I agree, he could have done a world of good, however, I don't know of one African American who benefited from him being General Counsel at Texaco. I guess that's why he left and went to Coca-Cola. Oh, you want to know what happened to the Task Force? Beats the hell out of me. Supposedly they were to find a new chair, I think they did, but the Task force was doing even more of nothing than before. Don't forget the Thirty-five million. I definitely should have gotten a refund from that part of the settlement. We should have sued whoever came up with that idea. Well maybe in theory it wasn't a bad idea because there probably would have been a substantial undercurrent if Texaco weren't on somebody's radar. But all in all it was a sham and a big fiasco. So I used to ask those status quo Negroes, "do you want the politically correct answer or the real story." I guess, not realizing, I was not really one of them, although dressed in my tuxedo they presumed I was, they would be taken aback by my reply. They would say, 'isn't it wonderful, these appointments'? I would say 'yeah, I guess, but even though I am not a lawyer by any means, there sure does appear to be a real conflict of interest with this General Counsel appointment'. I don't understand how they couldn't see that. I guess the scripture 'blind but do not see', was referring to these kinds of people. And even if they saw, no one who was in a position to say something did so. What could I do? There wasn't anything that I could do, because I had no one to go to. Where was I going to go, the NAACP, the Rainbow Coalition, the Newspaper? They were all praising Texaco. This is why I have such contempt. I mean, the courts should have been questioning the transition into this position after filing that favorable report for Texaco. I thought that he should have been disbarred because of the unethical nature of the deal. But like I said, I am not a lawyer. I do remember my colleague meeting with him prior to his appointment and had shared very confidential information with the now General Counsel of Texaco. During this time, my colleague had got caught in this crossfire with the management of our department and they wanted him gone. Somewhere during this time he had met with the Chair of the Task Force. Finally, he was forced out when they dissolved the Communications Department, which was the only way legally to get rid of him without it looking like retaliation. When I called and told him to guess who was the new General Counsel, he was so far off the mark I just had to laugh, even though there wasn't a damn thing funny about what I was about to tell him. Remember, he shared confidential information with this individual. God only knows what he told him, because he was there before me and was involved with the lawsuit both times. When I told him that his '*boy*', who was Chair of the Diversity Task Force, was now General Counsel, he hit the ceiling. I wouldn't be surprised if the Diversity Task Force Chair told them how to get rid of him. I remember hearing something to the affect, 'yeah, he knows a lot but he ain't got no case because he ain't got no documentation'. Then he was gone. After that, I was home alone. There wasn't anyone who could do anything about Texaco. Actually, everyone thought things were good. I still wonder if the report on Texaco was tainted. One can only speculate, but who really cares? However, if it looks like a fish and smells like a fish, guess what, it probably is a fish. During the chain of events, even the mailroom had even become all white. Even though I was alone, per se, I was still holding my own. I was not going to be caught in the middle of some garbage to jeopardize my employment. If they were going to get rid of me they were going to have to come correct. Now I can't blame the Chair for taking the position because I'm sure Texaco made him an offer he couldn't refuse, but where do we draw the line? Could not Texaco have found another qualified attorney in America for the position? Were there not any qualified Black attorneys that could have become General Counsel? It leads to speculation as to why him versus someone else? The other question is why do we as a people not question the ulterior motives that may exist. It was in the Newspapers, everyone knew who he was and where he came from. NAACP, Rainbow Coalition, where were they, why didn't they comment on it? Probably couldn't find the cameras. Someone had suggested to me that this deal might have been previously brokered during the settlement. Interesting, however it doesn't make it right.

We continue to be our own worse enemy, and those who supposedly are holding the banner of representation are so misguided as to what they consider is in our best interest, that they continue to lead us down this path of self-destruction.

I remember at the Christmas party how the *House Negro*es ignored me like I wasn't there. I am not talking about the regular ones; I am talking about the ones who had really benefited from this fiasco. What, you expected that they had changed the way they viewed us regular slaves? You know how everyone tries to get to speak to the CEO, well you should have seen their faces when they saw the CEO talking to little ole me. He asked me how things were going? You may ask why he would even bother to ask me that, but certain events transpired that changed my status in this game. And a few of those *House Negro*es were assigned to making it happen. So that's why he asked me how were things going? I looked over at them and looked back at the CEO straight in the eyes, just like he looked at me, and instead of giving him an earful about those useless biological creatures, I just said everything was pretty good. It was Christmas. It's interesting to watch how individuals would distance themselves from me like I was the bad guy. I was always going through that at Texaco. Then, when they would see the White people speak to me, especially the ones who they would regard as important, then it was 'Hi Peter', like we were friends or something. I hate phony, pretentious people, especially my own people. At least down in the Houston office, from the information I received from a colleague who worked down there, they wouldn't pretend at all about how they felt towards Black people. She would tell me stories of blatant racism. I said, "you have got to be kidding me!" She wasn't. I believe that is probably where the lawsuit for the women initiated. I don't know if it is true and my sole intent is to stick to the things I know for a fact, and the things I endured during this time. It was a mystery to many, after the lawsuit I was still around, especially after my colleague from the Communications Department got caught in the crossfire with Management. I was sure to be next, but like I said, I made it my personal business to be on time everyday and to never be absent. One would not think that never being late or absent would be enough to keep the wolves and/or sharks at bay, especially after the lawsuit, however, that basically was the only complaint my immediate supervisor, the Black female, ever had, was sometimes I was late. They could make an issue out of anything they so desired. It was just the opposite if you were in with the gang. When considering how most of the Blacks in the Company were being let go, even I had to wonder if I was next. I did however survive the aftermath that was taking place, or the covert operations that were materializing against us. It wasn't because I was so special or anything like that, it was mainly because I made a decision to go public about an incident shortly after the lawsuit. One of the CEO's initiatives after the lawsuit was to do an internal investigation, particularly for those individuals who gave depositions against Texaco. I'll tell you it sounded really great. Right! Wrong! You know when you come up with these ideas that sound good on paper they don't always turn out the way you might expect. So while the praise was growing for the new era in Texaco because of the few appointments and these initiatives, there was a whole slew of African Americans being displaced out of there. Even though those *House Negroes* sat back and didn't say or do anything, which I have little or no respect for, I must realize and accept, they probably didn't have the wherewithal to know any better, yet there was still this false image being portrayed about the progress of our people in Texaco. One must also realize that the backlash didn't end there, it also continued as one sought employment elsewhere. Sure Texaco gave you thirty days or maybe even sixty days to look within the Company, but they could have given you a year and the results would have been the same for us. I still can't say that I know of anyone of color who was successful in attempting that course of action for employment. So now you have to go out and find a job after being employed by Texaco, a company that was just sued by its Black employees. Who do you think was going to hire any Black from Texaco, whether you gave a deposition or not? Hell, if I was White I wouldn't hire you, and if I was Black and was in a position to recommend you for a position, I wouldn't, because I don't want no trouble round here on my plantation. We don't want no trouble for *massa* now. It was rough, but nobody thought about that. This is why it is so dangerous having these so-called Negroes praising Texaco or any company when there is something entirely different going on. Oh yeah, there were approximately three blacks that I can say for a fact that were seriously empowered; The Former EEOC, the Special Assistant to the CEO and the Chair of the Task Force, now General Counsel for Texaco. As for the rest of us, nothing but crumbs, the crumbs off of *massa's* table. Oh I almost forgot, the new

64

Omnsbud person. She was a black female. Probably the only one who deserved her position, and played a very strategic part in another situation that manifested before my final departure from Texaco. Anyway, that was the fantastic four and everyone was hallelujah, and all that. But my point is how quick we are satisfied with crumbs, and when we are satisfied with crumbs, it always has a major, adverse impact on the majority of our people. Shall we ever learn? Personally, I don't think so. Between all the theories out there about us and the effect of slavery upon us, and so on and so forth, I don't know if we shall ever overcome. I don't see the light at the end of the tunnel at this point. As long as there is such a fundamental difference between the ones who feel privileged and are not truly concerned about their fellowman or woman, we ain't gonna ever overcome a damn thing. Even though I have contempt for those individuals who sat at Texaco forever, I still felt responsible for their fate. I cannot just simply ignore what they were about to encounter going back out into the workforce. The other part that I find interesting is that the ones who were walking around like they were so damn important, didn't even have any formal education past high school. I guess that may have been why they were scared to say anything, because they knew that it would be hard to find another good plantation like Texaco's Corporate Headquarters. So, as *the brightest and the best* became the new corporate slogan, they were definitely not included. Part of me says serve their useless *asses* right. They got just what they deserved, especially after considering how they used to try and act all high and mighty around me. 'See ya, wouldn't wanna be ya', as they say in the streets. There is an old saying in life that goes something like, 'be careful who you step on, on the way up, because they are gonna be the same people you see on your way down'. So very true. So, while I was watching them being escorted out, or about to be escorted out, it was like watching, how they say on death row, 'dead man walking'. This was probably the first time in my life my degree had paid dividends, even if it was almost twenty years later. Not as far as finding a job equivalent to my educational background, that is another story, even though I have to confess that I never wanted to go to college in the first place, and all I really wanted to do was play in the NBA. I always knew that corporate wasn't for me. However, with a degree I was always assured I could get a job. I always knew that the workplace was for slaves and I guess the only way out of the Ghetto was to play ball or be an entertainer. I never thought about writing a book, at least not like this. So when they came up with the formula for the lawsuit, part of it was to compare you with a white employee with the same credentials, in the same position. And of course they couldn't find one white boy who had a degree and was where I was. They couldn't explain it away. That's why when I began mentoring and speaking to high school students, I would always emphasize the importance of education. I would explain to them how it is important, not just to have a good job, but more importantly to be able to handle yourself intellectually. I would explain how it's cool to be able to maintain your street vernacular, but how it was just as important to be able to interface intelligently with the people you work for and with. Let me tell you one thing, when I began writing those memos to the CEO, what I wrote was lethal, grammatically correct and to the point. He had no choice but to respect what I wrote, not because he really cared, but if it was to ever come back, it could be his worst nightmare. And if it could be that for him, then make no mistake, whoever was responsible for me writing the memo was going to have their head handed to them. That is why the memo I wrote that catapulted me into the newspaper changed everything. I knew, as they say in the street, I had to be tight with everything I wrote and everything I did. There was no room for mistakes. One mistake and I was history. For the first time in the twenty years after I graduated from college, I can actually say I was glad that I went, because I knew that by taking up this fight, if I didn't have the education I would not have survived the backlash that was taking place at Texaco. I also read the Wall Street Journal everyday. It was like my *Corporate Bible*, as I used to refer to it as such. It made me sharper than all my enemies. As far as I was concerned, if you weren't reading The Wall Street Journal you couldn't challenge me on any issue dealing with Corporate. I guess they can use this as a testimonial for their newspaper. Trust me, if I wrote anything that was grammatically incorrect I would have been destroyed. I conclude by saying that with the Grace of God, combined with my education, majoring in Economics and Management, I was able to not only survive, but fight tooth and nail after the lawsuit was settled. There were problems still, but I didn't know that I was about to be thrust into the spotlight by a newspaper article that was about to be written concerning another racial episode that I was the focal point of. There is a little secret that I would like to share. Although I was educated and I carried my Book of Psalms with me daily and would read the Wall Street Journal everyday of the work week, what really gave me the ability to carry on in this ruthless environment was the fact that I zipped up my boots and returned back to my roots. That's right, I went back to the 'Hood'. Took things back to the streets. I know many of you may be wondering why would I feel the need to go back to the 'Hood', to the Streets. What would I possibly find out there? I'll tell you what! I found real people, real problems, real life, and real love. And understand this, I didn't go out during the daylight hours. I would walk the streets at night. That's right, at night! If this was an autobiography I would take you through a journey and would have named this book The Life and Times of Pete Sherrill, however, this is about a segment in time and more about my people and the fraud that is and has been perpetrated upon us by our own people. Anyway, there was a time when the streets were a part of my life, and I went back there to get the edge I used to have. At night there is no room for the weak and frail. I used to say to those *House Negro*es in Texaco, I bet you couldn't find one of them in the streets of Harlem after dark. Personally, I loved Harlem at night. I used to ride the subway late at night, not worried about a damn thing. I was bad, not in the sense of crime, but bad because nobody would step to me. I was built like a rock, and that was all there was to it. So, I went back to get that fire. To be perfectly honest, there is not that much difference between the streets and the halls of Corporate America. If you don't watch your back you will end up with a knife in it. I went back to the streets to remember how to watch my back. I can say, because I went back, that when it came time to talk to these kids in middle and high school, I was able to command the attention and respect from all of them. Plus, when they found out that I had recorded a demo CD and went by the name of THOR (The Original Rock) and they saw the CD cover, how diesel, (that means built) I was, they would always pay attention to what I had to say. When I would tell them I am from the *Projects of Money Earnin Mount Vernon*, and if it wasn't for my education, I probably would have been dead or in jail, they understood that. I went on to tell them, how in corporate I was able to handle all my business and would read the newspapers that the CEO's and Senior VP's would read, and could hold conversations with them about the latest acquisitions in Corporate America and still talk to my people about who was the nicest on the court in basketball and why one rapper was superior to another. They really respected that. For me, reaching our youth became my most important goal. Still is till this day. As we continually struggle to teach our children the importance of a good education, they are seeing how corny, self-serving and unrealistic the ones who are preaching to them are. One thing you can rest assured of is that they can spot a phony a mile away and in a minute. They can tell as soon as you shake their hand and how you greet them. And as rap progresses and transcends all demographics and ethnicities, the less and less you *House Negroes* will be able to reach our youth. They don't want to be like you, brown-nosing, and kissing somebody's ass to exist. I   thank God for that. I just hope that they can be made aware of what is important to survive in this society, because the only thing that is for sure is the fact that the system is spending more money on prisons than for education.

People didn't understand that these white folks were angry about this settlement. They wanted blood. They even hated the CEO for settling. I mean, the white people who used to speak to me just outright stopped. I was like, the hell with you too. You know that since I was in street mode my response was significantly different. Boy, I sometimes still think I should write a clean and raw street version of this book. Like I said, I was pumping iron everyday, and if I wasn't worried about anyone in the street, I damn sure wasn't worried about anybody in Texaco. Trust me. My attitude was basically, if you want some of this come and get some of this. People used to ask me at times, 'what exactly do you do at Texaco'? I used to smile because I used to walk around the building whenever I felt like it. I used to visit people to see how they were doing. When their boss would come out they would look at me and just say hello. *'Respect for the individual'* was the other new slogan. And if you disrespected me you were gonna have a problem. I used to say to people that the CEO was the warden, but I was running the prison.

Actually, I was having fun in the jungle of Corporate America. I was going for my daily run every afternoon, then take a nice hot shower in the men's locker room, then afterwards have lunch. I guess you may think that is a bit much, but hell, I wasn't doing anything different than the Lawyers and Senior Level Executives were doing. It got to the point that the lawyers and me were on mutual speaking terms. They would ask me if I went jogging this afternoon and how many miles did I run today. The answer was always five or six. They would say things like, 'you really look good out there'. Much respect. I must admit that is probably the only thing I really miss at Texaco, those wonderful trails and hills in the Purchase/Rye-Brook area of Westchester County, the upper class, where homes cost well over a million dollars back then. I used to wonder how I would ever be able to afford a house like that unless I played ball or was an entertainer. Not that I wanted to live next door to them but I wanted to be afforded the opportunity to be in a position to own a house like that. I knew that as long as I was working for Texaco, or for that matter, any other corporation, that would never happen, given the cultural climate of discrimination in America, and Corporate America, that is still alive and well in 2007. As long as we are entertaining and playing sports, then it is acceptable for us to be in those types of neighborhoods, in those types of homes, but it is a rarity, professionally, for us to be in that classification from a business standpoint. That's what I have a problem with. I knew as I jogged along those beautiful trails, beautiful houses and fabulous

Corporations along Westchester Avenue, that I would never have the opportunity of being employed by any of these Corporations after all the hell I was raising up in Texaco. Hell, I didn't even know who I could put down for a reference. No matter if the CEO was saying that there would be no retaliation, no backlash, there was a price to pay that was going to have to be paid, if not now, definitely later. But I will tell you this, and this is especially for you *House Negro*es. When I joined this lawsuit against Texaco and stood up under fire during the deposition, for the first time in my life I felt like I really was somebody. You know that saying about standing up for something, well I'm here to tell you that it is so true. There is nothing like it. I was changed for life. I mean, it was, and still is, a great feeling. People still remember that lawsuit even though they are totally clueless how it ended, or what really happened. Freedom, liberation, purpose, and promise is what I felt. When you stand up and take that oath swearing to tell the truth the whole truth and nothing but the truth so help you God, and you do just that, it is incredible, when you know you are standing up for what is absolutely right. For you so-called Christians, try to practice what you preach. Have some faith, and trust God. For if God be for you who, who can stand against you? Oh ye of little faith. Easier said then done. You talk the talk but when it's time to take up the cross and walk the walk you all are a bunch of chickens. Hell, I had everything to lose. My first child had been born when I became part of this lawsuit that initially wasn't even meant for so-called people like me. Don't want anyone to forget that part of the beginning of this lawsuit. I might have made out a lot better if I would have sat there and said or did nothing, like the majority of you. But I thank God for the experience of his grace and power. Because there were times that only God was my refuge. There wasn't anyone else who could help me sustain the energy necessary to take on Goliath. I grew closer to God, and for that I am grateful. I learned he will never leave you alone when you stand up for truth and justice. How do you think Mandela was able to sit in the prisons of South Africa for so long fighting against Apartheid? Never yielding to the ever-present oppressor. You see, I believe that when you stand up for something righteous, God is there watching. You have to believe that. If you don't, then you will never make it through the difficult and trying times. But, man oh man, what a feeling, when God is on your side. Nothing and no one can stand in your way. Nothing and no one can turn you around as that ole spiritual the Negroes were singing while marching across the bridge to meet their oppressors face to face. Yeah, back then they were *Colored.* Don't matter. They knew what they were facing and they knew they were standing up for what was right and believed God was on their side. Faith! Those Negroes had faith! They trusted God. Maybe you *House Negro*es think that they didn't know any better, but I'll tell you this, they knew enough to know that what the White man was doing to them wasn't right. I thank God they did what they did. I thank God they had the courage to do what they did, because if they didn't, you can't even begin to imagine what things would be like in this country. There wouldn't be a Black on the Supreme Court, even if he is talking against Affirmative Action and anything Black. Boy oh Boy, I wish Malcolm was here to say a few choice words to him. If those Colored Negroes didn't do what they did, stand up for truth and justice, all those people running across our borders from oppressive regimes and politics, seeking freedom, probably wouldn't have a damn place to run to. So when you come over to this country remember one thing, many people died, shed their blood and fought hard for the freedom that you take for granted when you come here to America. When you see a Black person struggling in this country, remember that the war for freedom and equality still continues. Before you are so ready to judge African Americans based on the stereotypical propaganda, think twice, because it was the African Americans who made it possible for you to be able to bypass the racial inequalities and brutalities that existed when segregation was the practice and law of this land. The next time you vote, remember Martin Luther King Jr. How dare you come here and look down upon my people. You know, I learned the truth is a bitter pill to swallow and when you tell it, or if you dare to write it, those who it encompasses or addresses will often be offended by it. So do I dare not to tell it because it will offend? If I dare not to tell the truth then why the hell should I even bother to write this book? After joining the Lawsuit I was able to walk tall and proud because I knew what I was doing was right. I knew that standing up for what's right was good. So I hope all of you who continue to sit there and say nothing may gain some inspiration or some backbone. For all those domestic Negroes who sat there at Texaco for all those years being exploited and obviously knowing they were being exploited, because as soon as the judgment was decided you came out crying about how you have suffered the most and should get the most money, get the hell away from me. How dare you come out saying you deserve the most money, for what? Someone really needs to put you all out of your misery. Oh I said that already. Well it really needs saying again so you can see how sickening you are. If things were so bad, then why didn't you say something? Do something? I guess you were waiting for Moses to deliver you from the grip of Pharaoh. You know, when I think of what could have happened to me and my new born daughter when I decided to become part of this Class Action against Texaco, and how I could have lost my job and possibly jeopardize my newborn daughter's future, and I think of those individuals at Texaco who sat there for all of those years, I really and truly have contempt towards them. By the same token, I have to realize that this was some serious life-changing event, sometimes with no point of return. I guess if it's not in you it's not in you. But don't find some backbone after the fact. That is all I'm saying. They had us Blacks fighting over the money like animals. It was disgusting. But that was because those self-serving good for nothing *House Negroes* made it that way. You know they have a way of bringing chaos to everything. I really believe that if the lead plaintiffs were still around after the Lawsuit was won, a lot of the ills that had taken place would not have occurred. The media would have still been there, the attorney's would have still been there, the Chair for the Task Force probably wouldn't have gotten the position as General Counsel, and the aftermath would not have been an aftermath. Well maybe there would have still been an aftermath but it would have been done under much more scrutiny. There would have been someone there to say, it looks like Texaco is retaliating against their Black employees. You see how it could have been extremely different? I can't say I blame the lead plaintiff for going to write her book, but since she wasn't there after the lawsuit, there was so much that she was not aware of that was going on internally at Texaco. There was not anything she could do about it since she was no longer an employee there. The other lead plaintiff eventually died and he wasn't more than forty plus. I believe the stress from the lawsuit had something to do with his death. I may be wrong, but I do know enough to know that stress kills. Even though I really didn't get to know him until the lawsuit, I have decided, as you may have seen in the beginning of this book, to give a special tribute to him for everything that he did to stand up and fight this giant. I say to him *'Rest in Peace for the Truth is finally being told'*. I hope he can see me writing this testament. Actually, another good friend of mine also died recently, and I know she was going through a lot after she left Texaco. Let me tell you, leaving Texaco was not easy for a lot of people. Even when I decided it was time for me to leave, I wrestled for a great length of time before I finally said the hell with it. After I said the hell with it, it was a tremendous relief. I don't know if the goal of the lead plaintiff who passed away was to ever come back to Texaco to work for the new and improved Goliath or whether he was coming back to challenge Texaco to ensure they were doing the right thing. I think he wanted to ensure that Texaco was doing the right thing. I guess it didn't matter after the Lawsuit was settled because Texaco made sure neither of the lead plaintiffs were around to ensure anything. That strategy allowed Texaco to continue with business as usual. They bought the Chair of the Task Force and that was probably the last obstacle to total control. So for all those who sat there like good domestic Negroes, their stay of execution was just about to be up.

You know, many may wonder why I am so adamant about the lack of awareness or complacency that we have come to reflect and accept ever since the loss of our two most prominent leaders, Malcolm and Martin. I just want you to know that I realize that undertaking this enormous mission wasn't easy by any means, however, anything worthwhile usually isn't. The price tag of this Lawsuit and the destruction that followed afterwards can never be estimated. Not just in terms of the effect it had on Blacks but the effect it had on everyone, including the Corporation. I myself was personally responsible for the destruction of a White employee who caught my wrath and indignation. I never in my life knew what it was like to see someone broken, except for in the streets, but never because of me. Stripped of all his responsibility. And the newspaper wanted his name for the story, but Texaco refused to give it to them. I didn't want to give it to them either. And I didn't. But the things he said to me had to be dealt with, so hence, another memo to the CEO. As I discussed what happened during my interview with this individual with my colleagues for the Internal Investigation mandated by the CEO, they were outraged and asked me what did I do? I said nothing. They were surprised, and my partner said he would have walked out, someone else said they would have responded back fiercely. I said, "I know." But I kept my cool and continued on with the interview. God knows that I wanted to reach across that table and break his *fuckin* neck! (OOPS)! Considering the shape that I was in, I could have, believe me. If this were in the streets, he would have been a dead man. That's how serious what he said was. When I spoke with my buddy from the newspaper, he asked me about the Internal Investigation and did I know anything about it. I said yeah, I just got finished talking to one of the people appointed by the CEO to conduct the interview. When I began to tell him what happened, he said, "You have got to be kidding me!" I said, 'nope'! He then asked me if I had any proof? I said, I sent a memo to the CEO and they were conducting an investigation into what I wrote. He then asked for the memo, I said, "no man I can't do that!" He responded, "Pete, come on man, have I ever let you down!" I said, 'no'! He replied again, " Pete, let me get this story!" I remember waking up in the middle of the night after I went through the interview that afternoon, about four or five in the morning and woke up and said, "OH HELL NO!" and began writing this memo. Well, I finally agreed, even though that's not exactly what I said. So I had someone else fax over the memo to my boy at the newspaper and let me tell you, the shit was about to hit the fan! This was so powerful that Texaco sent its representatives over to stop the story from coming out. That's right, this story was about to bring Texaco to its knees. This is when and how I became an integral part of the post Texaco Lawsuit era. My deposition against Texaco was important, but since the tapes emerged and they decided to settle before having their day in court, my deposition didn't really matter. I guess if the CEO didn't order that Internal Investigation, I would not have as interesting a story to write about. Maybe I would, but now this was personal. Oh yeah, you know because of the settlement, Texaco was allowed to admit to no wrongdoing. So as far as they were concerned there wasn't anything wrong with the way they were running the company. Imagine! I wonder who agreed to that? I would have said 'see you in court'. But what do I know. A post war era was about to begin and no one had any idea what was about to happen. I will tell you this, there is nothing more powerful than the truth. So if you are telling the truth, don't even worry about it. There is justice out there. I'm not going to lie and say that when this post war was about to begin I wasn't praying a whole lot, because when that article ran, and it ran in the Sunday edition, where everyone would see it, I knew I was fired. So did my other partner who added his comments about the abuse that was still going on in Texaco. One may wonder if it was worth the risk writing this memo and giving it to the newspaper. But how could I live with myself if I let him disrespect me like that, and say nothing. I guess that is the fundamental difference between myself, and those who sat at Texaco for decades saying nothing, and those who continue to sit in these corporations mute. There is a price to pay if you sit and say or do nothing and there is a price to pay if you do say something. I decided long ago that my dignity and integrity were not for sale and Texaco was about to find that out. It wasn't Texaco's fault per se, however this individual was chosen to conduct this interview and was from the Human Resources Department. You would think that someone who had been with the company for so many years and in HR would know not to say anything derogatory to any individual. That just goes to show the mentality that existed in Texaco. So the war was about to begin. One thing that I wasn't aware of before I let that memo end up at the newspaper, was that they were going to have to check with Texaco to verify my story. When my boy at the newspaper called me and said his Editor had to speak with Texaco first, I said, "what the hell do you mean?" "If I had known that, I would have never given you the story." He said, "Pete don't worry, I got your back." Man I tell you, this was getting messy. If you think this wasn't serious, let me tell you this, My friend at the newspaper wasn't even allowed to write the story because Texaco felt that he had been too outspoken in his articles about the Lawsuit and other matters pertaining to Texaco. It was then I realized that the press was not an independent source of information and was really controlled by corporate interest. By the time Texaco's representatives got finished with the newspaper whose

Headquarters, by the way, was right down the street from Texaco's headquarters on that strip of illustrious corporations, they, damn near killed the impact the story would really have had. Nevertheless, the truth has its way of rising to the surface. So there it is, everything on the line, especially my ass and my neck, everything. My future that didn't exist at Texaco, everything. Was I scared? Yes and no. I do know that it was the right thing to do no matter what. I say that now because of the way things turned out. However, if they had turned out the way they did with my fellow colleague in the lawsuit I probably wouldn't be saying this. I probably would be even angrier than I already am. I'm telling you, those individuals who were in this Class Action were worthless. It really made me wonder if it was worth the fight. Would I do it all again? Honestly, yes I would, because in actuality, it wasn't about them, it was about what was right, in spite of them. Actually, I didn't join for them anyway. I did it because I felt as though I didn't have any other choice. So even though the Lawsuit initially wasn't for 'people like me', in the end I am glad that it did become a Class Action so I could be part of this process. If there weren't a Class Action Lawsuit going on at the time, I would have been forced to eat Texaco's shit. You know, when I think about it, it wasn't really Texaco's shit, it was the bullshit of the management of the department I was in that set this whole thing off. Granted it was also part of the corporate culture, so who is to blame? I still say and insist unequivocally, that those who sat there for all those decades cost us much in the end. Those domestic, complacent, docile, Negroes, not just at Texaco, but everywhere they are, cost us much. They cost us our pride and integrity, our dignity and respect. Hell, if we don't respect ourselves, how the hell can we expect someone else to respect us? So here I am, a dead man walking, at least that is what I thought. It is interesting as I reflect on this episode in my life, how my spirituality was a huge part of this whole encounter. It is hard when all you have to rely on and depend on, and trust in, is God. But it is so rewarding in the same breath to know that it was just that trust which saw you through. You must understand that when I reference God, it is much different than those traditional, "We shall overcome Christians." I'm more like David, going to battle. "Lord, destroy all mine enemies." "Make them my footstool." "Rise up and hear the right oh Lord." 'The Psalms baby', especially the 27th Psalms. " The Lord is my light and salvation whom shall I fear? The Lord is the strength of my life, of whom shall I be afraid? When the wicked, even my enemies and my foes, came upon me to eat up my flesh, they stumbled and fell. Though a host should encamp against me, my heart shall not fear. Though war should rise against me, in this will I be confident." If there is ever a book you want to read that will bring you from the depths of hell into victory, read Psalms. I'll stake my life on it. Actually I did stake my life on it. It was the Psalms that I continually read all my days after college. There is no book like it in the entire Bible. In the book of Psalms David exhibits a faith, and a love of the Lord that is undeniably second to none. Job's faith was awesome, but David's faith was more practical. More human. I used to like when he knew he really made a mess of everything. And I'll tell you, there were times in my life when I used to make a mess of everything. Well not everything, but I used to mess things up pretty bad, and all I could do was call on God to get me the hell out of whatever mess I was in. I used to be a very angry man. I hated everyone. I hated my family, and I wouldn't even speak to my mother. I was hostile and dangerous. If I had a gun, God knows for sure that I would have killed someone a long time ago. I am so glad I have changed. He changed me, wretched soul that I was. But that still doesn't mean that I have to accept those useless *House Negro*es. I still hate them! I hate them all the way back to the continent of Africa from which I was taken. I still blame them and I always will! I don't give a damn what anyone says. I know that sounds narrow-minded, but part of it is due to the attitude and disposition Africans have towards Black Americans. They really need to recognize that we made it possible for them to even come here of there own free will. They are clueless as to the sacrifices it took for the slightest possibilities for them to even exist here in America today. They don't have any idea how many lives were lost because of their inability to protect our land in Africa, and they have the god damn gall to think that they are superior to us when they get here. I have a little story I'll share later on in this book about an encounter with an African over here talking about how wonderful it is over there, but for now I am on my way to meet the enemy to explain why I joined this Action and filed this petition against Texaco.

Chapter 6

The Internal Investigation

You can call it what you want, damage control, good public relations or just an attempt to make Texaco look like a warm sensitive organization. Regardless of the reasons, it was

ordered by the CEO, and a investigation was going to happen. There were just the three of us left out of the five from Corporate Headquarters who gave depositions against Texaco, because the two lead plaintiffs were strategically removed. I knew it wasn't going to be long before I got the call to participate in this charade. Sure enough, the call came on behalf of the CEO from the Human Resources Department. Now I had the opportunity to opt out, if I so desired, but the CEO really wanted to get to the bottom of it all. I guess it was easier to deal with those who weren't the lead plaintiffs, and it continues to make me wonder if the same measures would have taken place if they were still there. Reluctant to participate in this process, I knew that if I didn't go it would look like there was no justification to my deposition. I couldn't allow that. So I agreed to participate. I went to a conference room in the Human Resources Department to meet this individual, whose status in the Company I had no idea of at the time. All I knew was that they wouldn't entrust this to just anyone. He sure looked the part of that life long company man, so I knew I had to be careful with my responses to his questions. You know those HR people, they ask questions that mean something entirely different. He was in his mid to late fifties I would guess. He introduced himself to me and we began with the small talk. All in all, I was there for several hours just to give a perspective of how in depth this process was. And now what we all have been waiting for! Somewhere in the midst of our Q&A it got very personal. He began insulting me, making derogatory comments like, "I guess you are going to go buy yourself a Mercedes now with the money from the Lawsuit." I was like, "no, not really." That's when I knew I was in for some trouble. Then, he went on to say, "you know, I don't see what the big deal is with calling Blacks the N word." "Where I grew up we used to call them the N word all the time and it wasn't a big deal, they didn't seem to mind." One thing you have to remember is, the tapes that emerged from this Class Action, had Senior Level Executives on tape calling Blacks, niggers, and all types of racial slurs like porch monkeys, etc. I looked at him in astonishment. I was like, oh hell no! No he didn't say that to me, looking me right in my eyes and straight in my face. No he didn't! He basically was calling me a nigger to my face and was saying he didn't see anything wrong with that. I was thinking of how to come back and respond, but I knew that if I did I could possibly be in serious trouble. So I decided to sit back and act like everything was cool. I started rubbing my Abe Lincoln style beard that I discovered in my collegiate days. Actually it was more like the Moses look, which they used to call me on Campus. Anyway, I sat there for the next few hours and continued the interview. It ended on a cordial note, but if this were in the streets, I'm telling you, I would have really broken his *fuckin* neck!

Oh, I know all you *House Negro*es are probably saying what barbaric language, such violence. But you know what? Fuck you too! You would come out with some type of rationalization and/or justification, or turn the other cheek, forgive them for they know not what they do bullshit. Sorry, go read another book. This is exactly why I am writing this book. Not so much about what happened in Texaco and it's discriminatory practices, but how you people allowed Texaco to exist like this for decades, generations! Sorry, disrespecting me is not an option! Anyone who is disrespected should never accept it. And I am here to tell it. To let everyone who is somebody know, you don't have to accept being disrespected, because if you do you are making it worse for your children and their future. So get over it. I believe in the previous chapter I said I felt bad about this white individual being broken and castrated. Now that I truly remember the arrogance and defiance and how he felt justified condoning the use of the N word by the executives of Texaco, to hell with him and all the rest of those racists bastards! Previously, I had actually forgotten what had happened for the moment, and basically, only remembered my picture and my famous quote about finding one white male. I forgot about the fact that the article was pursued so rigorously by the newspaper and Texaco attempting to kill it, because they were scared as all hell for another incident to come out, especially during an investigation called for by the CEO, where his representative called one of the plaintiffs in so many words a Nigga! again. Texaco was scared to death. Before I left the conference room he asked me was there anything I would like for him to tell the CEO? I was like, "yeah right!" He replied, "no, really." I remember telling him to tell the CEO not to believe everything those who advise him are telling him, because they are not telling him everything that is really going on. I guess it was because when we had our gathering in the auditorium, our time to heal, executives, who were addressing the employees kept saying, "we didn't know." I say how the hell could you not know something like that? The real fact was that you didn't give a damn. The other fact, which is so very true, is that no one ever said anything. If no one is saying anything then how the hell is someone suppose to know? So my question again becomes, is it Texaco's fault or ours? I say it is those *god damn House Negro*es. I'm telling you and I will continue telling you. The damage they cause because of complacency, ignorance, fear, whatever else they lack in character, has, and still does, cause a tremendous amount of damage to our race. I believe it's irreparable damage! I hope not, I pray not, however!

Like I said, it was about four o'clock in the morning, I woke up and said "Oh hell no!" I found some paper, got a pen, went to the dining room table and began to reconstruct what transpired in that interview with a memo to the CEO. I don't remember if I had it typed by a friend of mine or if I typed it myself, all I knew was that I was going straight to the top with this. Then again, everything I was writing was going straight to the top. But this was going to be unlike anything else I've ever written, except this doctrine I'm now putting together. I guess the rest is history. All hell broke loose when my boy from

Chicago who worked for the newspaper got his hands on this story. He was constantly putting Texaco out there like that. I remember during Black History Month how he wrote that everyone filled the auditorium to watch Winford Marsalis play his horn or when there was some type of special entertainment, with us dancing and/or singing, but when we had the forum to discuss diversity and race relations at Texaco, hosted by Gil Noble no less, from Like It Is on ABC, there weren't hardly any whites in the audience. Go figure. I guess as long as we sing and dance, I guess they are comfortable with us in that capacity. Just like back in the day, we could perform at the clubs but had to enter in the rear. Do you remember that? It got to the point that the CEO ordered the Senior Level Executives to attend our events. So when 'my brother' asked about the internal investigation, it was on. I'll tell you, the Press are like sharks, they can smell blood and they like it. And that's how I got my fifteen minutes of fame. But I'll tell you, if I knew that it would have to go through all the steps, like the story being run by Texaco first and how the press even entertained the representatives from Texaco who were trying to squash the story, I probably would have never sent it, especially since it went upstairs to the CEO first. I could have been executed for that. As I explained previously, the call was made to Texaco and after all was said and done the article rolled. I remember getting the call asking me if I saw the Sunday paper? I was in shock when I saw a small caption and a picture of myself with my famous quote underneath challenging Texaco to show me one white male with a double major in Management and Economics at a grade level equivalent to someone working in the mailroom. The real shock came after opening to the continuing part of the paper and there it was, a full-blown picture of myself on one side and the CEO on the other page. It was a huge article. A shot of the CEO on one page with the microphones in front of him at a press conference, and on the other side, a full picture of me that 'my brother' from the paper had taken of me coming down the Courthouse stairs in White Plains, New York, after the fairness hearings, my fresh clean cut, clean shaven corporate look and my Pierre Cardin suit. I'm trying to tell you, I was one of the best-dressed men at Texaco. You know that old saying they were promoting, 'dress for success'. Well I dressed the part, looked the part, and you couldn't tell me that one day I wouldn't be running Texaco. When I got to work that Monday I knew I wasn't getting past the front gate. I knew I was dead. Then when I went to the cafeteria that morning, there she was, the woman who puts up the news about the oil companies on the bulletin board right outside the cafeteria. The whole article, there wasn't any room for anything else. That's how long the article was. Everybody was looking at me, and it was like I was in the Twilight Zone or something. There were some people congratulating me. You know what else? They were White! I can't say that there were many Blacks that said much, if anything, to me, except for one that I can think of off hand. I remember him saying to me, "say it isn't so." He was shocked to see that I was earning this unimaginable minimum wage type of money at the

Corporate Headquarters of Texaco. He was actually a C.P.A. It shocked everyone, and embarrassed the hell out of Texaco. Even though Texaco lead the story, saying it was going to take time for things to change and give them a chance, when it got to the part about the N word, it didn't really have the impact it should have had, but it had enough where I became the one not to ever mess with. That's when I began 'running the prison'. It was a risk, but in the end it was worth taking. It could have turned out differently, easily, but it sure would have looked like retaliation. They tried to stop the story and almost succeeded. Again, there were attempts to get the individual's name, but I refused to do that. However, Texaco dealt with him and dealt with him swiftly. Word went around like a rocket. I never wanted it to turn out like that. I never wanted things to be this way. Maybe the EEOC was right, I should have never taken such a menial position within the organization. NOT! You do have to realize one thing, and that is I loved working for Texaco. Similar to the lead plaintiff, it wasn't until I felt betrayed that things went sour. I thought maybe it was me, but as I read some of the depositions, there were people who were treated far worse than I could have ever imagined. That's when I realized it wasn't me, it was the color of my skin. I always liked the color of my skin. I probably even felt that I was privileged because of my complexion. I mean, I do tan really nice and I always see white people trying to get tan like me. Seriously though, it was a sad day for me when I truly realized that it was the color of my skin. What a hurtful and painful feeling that was, when I realized that I had been racially discriminated against. You are never the same, ever. I remember walking into the Financial Planning Group that morning. No one said a word to me. Basically I was waiting for security to escort me out. As though it was my fault that I was discriminated against. Then it happened, out of nowhere, the CEO decided he was going to level the playing field for me. You know this wouldn't have even happened if it weren't for that article in the newspaper. The word I got was, "you tell Pete that I am going to level the playing field for him and if he messes up he is outta here! outta here!" Personally, I welcomed the opportunity and the challenge. So now, all of a sudden, the playing field is supposedly going to be level for me. What the hell was it before? Then I got the call from, guess who? The former EEOC, who has been promoted to some new position, but they still brought in somebody from the outside to head up the HR department, which he wanted to run. There was to be a meeting pertaining to the directives from the CEO with the former EEOC and the head of HR to discuss my career path on this newly found level playing field. WOW! I guess I ought to thank that racist bastard for sharing his views with me about calling us *niggas*, because if it wasn't for that and the article I would have been in the same position still, with the same complaints in all probability. So the meeting was scheduled, and I was instructed where to meet in the Human Resources Department. I walked in and shortly afterwards, here comes the former EEOC. As you may recall we sure had our differences, and he took the opportunity to let me have it. He started in on me, "I told you what you needed to do already and you didn't listen." I wanted to tell him that the advise you gave me was bullshit and wasn't worth a damn dime. But I knew I couldn't. Then the truth came out. "I'm not scared to talk one on one with you." I was like, where the hell did that come from? Then I remembered, his white colleague. Evidently the word was out not to speak to me without someone present to collaborate the story. Made sense I guess. I was wondering why my Black female supervisor always would talk to me with someone around, especially after I ripped her apart about my evaluation. So after letting me know that bit of information I let him ramble on about how this was all my fault. At first, I sat up in the chair in a confrontational posture, then, I remembered that if I blew this I was history. So I took his shit, for a little while at least. Shortly thereafter, one of the Senior Executives from the department came in the room. Boy was I glad when I saw it was someone I knew and was on a friendly basis with. You should have seen the look on the EEOC's face when that Senior Executive (of course he was white) addressed me by my first name and began talking with me about what I thought about this program I was about to go through. That *nigga* backed up off of me quick, fast and in a hurry. I'm telling you, that's how it was most of the time up there. Blacks would act like they didn't know me, and then when they would see how the white executives and other white employees would greet me, only then would they try to engage in a conversation or say hello. So for the most part I got along far better with the Whites than the Blacks. Sad but true. So I began telling him how I thought this was a great opportunity and I look forward to the challenge and the rest of that professional small talk. After that, things went very well after he left the room and me and my good buddy, the EEOC were alone again. He explained the process to me, how I was going to be evaluated and assigned a coach and a mentor at the Senior Level to help me with my development. I was now on the fast track of Texaco. I had arrived. I realized that standing up for what you believe in is far more rewarding than sitting on your ass for the rest of your life for a paycheck. How pathetic. Now there were two of us in this program, my colleague who had insisted that I join this Lawsuit, and myself. My colleague had already been introduced to the program before I was, probably because he had a longer history with the company and he was well known by all the executives. He also raised a lot of hell with the management of our department. I also realized he felt privileged to be the only one of the plaintiffs to be in this program. I admit I was curious how and why he was chosen, but I wished him no ill will. But now it was my turn and I was about to do my thing, and make the best out of this opportunity. That's all I ever wanted was the opportunity to showcase my skills and my intelligence. Now I was thrust into the big-time. It somewhat bothered me not knowing if they would have considered me for this program if that article hadn't run, and how sincere they really were given the nature of the article, but I really couldn't be consumed by what I felt personally. As they say, God works in mysterious ways.

And I guess he had a plan all mapped out, so to speak. Either way you look at it, I had arrived. Whether it was by plane, train or foot, I made it. I was going to make the best of this opportunity regardless, and I wasn't going to be the one to mess it up. What's interesting is that with a stroke of a pen Texaco could make whatever they wanted to happen, happen. That's power, and I wanted it. Yes I wanted money, but I wanted that power that those executives had. I wanted to be able to fly on the company jet when I was ready. I just wanted to play. That's all. I didn't just want to continue playing in the minor league. I always felt I was ready for the big leagues. I guess I just believed all that stuff that was written on my Degree. It really is impressive when you read it. However, in all honesty, I thought I could play pro ball and bypass all that corporate mumbo jumbo. You know, it's like when I did my first real research paper in college. I did it on Malcolm X and it was the first time I really ever applied myself to a project. Basically, I skated through college, except for one rough semester. Yeah, I had it like that. I was smart like that I guess. I did just enough to get by. But when I did that paper, I read almost every article in every magazine and cross referenced every cross reference. What a tremendous learning experience. I especially never forgot one thing that Malcolm said. "You are always in trouble when you have to rely upon your enemy for a job." It was when I graduated from college that I realized that I was going to be in trouble. But that's another story. This could have gone very different, and I never expected anything like this to transpire.

Personally, I wish that this could have happened without all the drama, without a Lawsuit of Racial Discrimination. Let me tell you, there is nothing gratifying about being discriminated against. Actually, it's a terrible feeling. It's dehumanizing. That's why I can't understand how anyone can sit around and accept being treated like that. I realize that getting paid is important, however, somehow I don't believe that the price for a paycheck should mean you have to sacrifice your integrity and dignity. When will these *House Negro*es wake up? Collectively they are destroying us. If you continue to sit back for years and years, this is the type of inequity you are preparing for our future generation. I guess as long as our leadership at the national level remains as inept as it is, we don't stand much of a chance. I ask, "has anybody seen my old friend Martin or Malcolm, can you tell me where they've gone". I say this because this is serious. This ordeal has definitely changed me forever. Yes, I am aware that we won the Lawsuit or the battle, but it was the war that I was more concerned about. And remember, if those tapes with those racial slurs were not unveiled, we would have been in an all out war, a long and ugly war. Recalling that this lawsuit initially was not for the Class, part of me now wishes that it wasn't, because of those useless, docile, pathetic *House Negro*es who sat there for all those years like good slaves. However, for this lawsuit initially to not be open to those who wanted to join because they were not in a certain classification within the organization, proved to be, as far as I was concerned, just as detrimental. This whole thing started out as self-serving. That is what still bothers me, even now, almost ten years later. It bothers me just as much as listening to some ignorant white person tell me that he doesn't see the problem with calling us *niggas.* As for myself, if I was not betrayed there wouldn't have been a need to seek out participation in this discrimination lawsuit. My point is that those who sat there, and those who were only concerned about this lawsuit for a select few are just as detrimental and destructive to our race as that ignorant white individual. There is no difference. I wonder if I too am guilty of self-servitude? Is betrayal enough to bring forth a charge of racial discrimination? You know this thing would have never happened if the woman who was the lead plaintiff remained on the fast track at Texaco. On the other hand, it made Corporate America take a real good hard look at its organizational charts. Even if betrayal isn't justification for a racial discrimination lawsuit, it sure is a high price tag to pay. So even if this started out with all the wrong intentions, in the end none of the other Corporations wanted to get hit with a Class Action Lawsuit like Texaco did. Actually, for the moment, while things were still hot, some organizations took this threat seriously. Many people are unaware that Coca-Cola was facing the same type of scrutiny. Would you care for some irony? After Texaco settled, Coca-Cola eventually hired our former EEOC and shortly afterwards the General Counsel followed suit. You remember, the one who used to be head of the Diversity Task Force, who said he could do so much more on the inside! What a joke! Actually it's disgusting. Then again, I can hear those misguided Negroes from god knows where, applauding, saying "isn't that wonderful." I've never seen such a group of clueless *fuckin* people.

So here I am being prepared for my indoctrination into the fast track of Texaco Inc. Step one begins with a psychological evaluation to determine where I would excel. Personally, I felt as though I was being psychoanalyzed to determine what the hell was my problem. There I was in midtown Manhattan, in some plush office talking to some Black man about this process. What's interesting is, when I spoke to my colleague who had already interviewed with this individual, his went a whole lot better than mine. After he finished with my colleague he offered to introduce him to his daughter. That should have been my first clue I was about to be had. I said mine went nothing like that. But having me isn't that easy. Again, I just went through with the process and was being as cooperative as I could be. I was playing the game. Or was I? I went through these social evaluations, mathematical concepts and a host of other evaluations. It took all day. After all was said and done, we went over my chart. We discussed my strengths and weaknesses, and reached certain conclusions as to where I would probably excel. I was amazed to find that I had many attributes that were characteristic of a CEO. After the testing and the results were finally in, it was time for the big meeting with the former EEOC, my Department Head, who I basically accused of being a racist in a memo to the CEO, my Coach who was going to be assigned to me and the psychologist. Once again my colleague met with the gang before me, got this fabulous evaluation from the psychologist, and was on his way. It didn't quite work out that way for me. You see, I wrote memos and I was the new troublemaker. When the meeting commenced, make no mistake about it, it was payback time. They roasted my *black ass*. The psychologist was not saying anything in my favor. The EEOC and my Department Head had the floor and that was how this meeting was going to go. I tried to get my thoughts in regarding this process but they weren't trying to hear anything I was saying. I'll tell you, thank God for lunch. They needed some raw meat to eat! I remember breaking for lunch and was in the bathroom at the same time with the psychologist. I was wondering what happened to having the attributes of a CEO? When they asked me what I thought about the report and I tried to mention that I was intrigued by the fact of having the attributes of a CEO, they were not trying to hear that. We went round and round for a while, then I finally decided to get off the merry-go round. I became a yes man, maybe even a good House Negro. Not! I just started agreeing with everything they were saying and they were happy. They were like, "now you got it!" I laugh now, but it wasn't funny then. I realized that compromising was necessary if I was going to get to the next phase of this matrix. Afterwards, I had my first meeting with my Coach. We went downstairs, somewhere private, so we could talk. I remember him saying to me, "man I had no idea they were going to do you like that. You must have really pissed someone off." I smiled proudly because I knew I did more than just piss someone off, I had managed to piss everyone off. I crucified them. I was implementing my readings of the Psalms on their *asses*. Can I say that and still use Psalms? Don't want those holier than thou Christians calling me a blasphemer. I was literally trying to destroy anyone who I considered my enemy. I'm telling you, it was no joke once I decided to go to war. I studied war a lot after college. I read Eisenhower's Diaries, Patton volumes I & II, and if there were a III, I would have read that also. I really could identify with Patton, but I loved McArthur, American Cesar. I began to understand what Martin Luther King Jr. meant when he said " I shall study war no more." It is dangerous when you study war all the time. You become like the characters you read. All I was reading were about Generals, Leaders of America, Conquerors, skilled and highly intellectual men who feared God and had a deep spirituality. They were fascinating, because they were real. They existed. I remember one memo I sent about my department head to the CEO with all the back up documentation of my previous memos to him regarding the organizational chart of our department and how there wasn't one African American in a decision making capacity in the entire department, thus questioning his position regarding African Americans at Texaco. And you wonder why they roasted my skinny behind that afternoon. I had documents that I had sent two years prior, regarding my career at Texaco. Yep, it was on. I wasn't taking any prisoners and I wasn't holding back anything. I was ruthless. I was not playing with any of them. You mess with me, and you better believe a memo was going to surface like a scud missile. I was launching nuclear warheads. I was setting up paper trails like a wick for dynamite. I would go to my boys, "give me a match" and act like I'm lighting the fuse from my paper trail headed straight for the powder keg. Sad to say, I was having fun blowing people up. My interviewer from the internal investigation wanted to apologize to me and the CEO's assistant contacted me to see if I wanted to meet with him. I flat out refused. This was not the figurehead Black assistant that was brought in by the CEO after the settlement to pacify those *House Negroes*. This was a real assistant that was brought in to eventually run an Operating Division. Understand the difference? Don't you know that white racist bastard called me and wanted to see me, and then one day took it upon his self to come my office. I called upstairs and asked why he came to my office? They said he really wanted to apologize that's all. I said he would not want to apologize if he was at retirement, because he personally told me if he didn't have to hang in there for a few more years he would tell a few people where to go. Anyway, I let it go and I accepted his apology, and you could see that whatever they did to him it was killing him. Now maybe you can begin to see why they couldn't wait to get their hands on this here little colored boy. Yeah they wanted me bad, but by the end of the meeting we were all on the same page. This was my beginning of learning diplomacy. My background in Management and Economics were no longer of importance. I was in a new game. I had to learn and learn fast. The playing field was leveled and I had the ball. They finally gave me the ball, and it was totally up to me whether I was going to win or lose, fail or succeed. For that I have to thank my Coach. My Coach who was assigned to me told me 'straight up' like this. He explained to me that when he got the call his first question was, do we really want to help this guy or are we just going through the motion. He said the plan was and is to really help me. Personally, I was shocked, but I think everyone had a stake in me being successful. I mean, if I succeeded then everyone looked good. Actually, this was shaping up to be a win-win situation all across the board, if I played my cards right. Another interesting point was how they selected my Coach. He was a former professional football player for the New England Patriots, and he was a real cool brother. I mean he knew all the famous players in the NFL. Mean Joe Green, Franco Harris, Drew Pearson, you name it he knew them, played with them and still hung out with them. I truly admired him. This was going to be the beginning of a really great relationship and a testament to the type of company Texaco could have and should have always been. As I sit here and reflect on how this could have turned out, totally opposite from this great new beginning, I truly thank God for seeing me through this storm. As I also reflect on this entire ordeal, I am still attempting to come to grips as to why, when we were damn near in the twenty-first century, well over one hundred years after the Emancipation Proclamation, and at the same token, two generations, forty years after the death of Malcolm and Martin. Ironic isn't it? Why are we still fighting this fight against racial injustice?

People sometimes ask me do I believe things are going to get better? My favorite answer to them is if things were going to get better the final chapter in the Bible would not be Revelations. Revelations, the ultimate battle, basically because there is nothing left that can be done to change this course of destruction that man is headed down. Personally, I must have read Revelations a hundred times or more. Amongst my books of Generals that I have digested, I must include the Holy Bible, because that is the book that kept me from going in the wrong direction, to choose love vs. hate, to choose forgiveness vs. revenge. I remember when I graduated from college and was looking for a job, how I hated that whole process that one is subjected to when applying for a job. It was a horrible experience. I remember saying to myself, "damn, if I'm catching this kind of hell trying to get a job, imagine what my people, especially the brothers on the street with maybe only a high school education are going through." Hell, they don't stand a chance. That's when I remember my report in college on Malcolm X. Again, 'you are always in trouble when you have to go to your enemy for a job.' He sure wasn't lying. My question is, how could that still be, after everything we went through during the Civil Rights Movement? There was no reason for me to be having to fight such a battle in or with Texaco. We really need to take a serious look and see why that was and still is the case today. I remember when I came out of college in 1980, those god damn white males, had the *motha fuckin* nerve to be crying reverse discrimination, imagine that! Then Ronald Reagan became president, riding in on his white horse to save White America with Reagonomics, which damn near destroyed the American economy, and Affirmative Action was dead, compounded by twelve years of Republicanism. Or was it? Maybe it was the Democratic Party who left us out there like that. Actually, I believe they all felt that Affirmative Action had to be stopped. The Democrats abandoned us just like they continue to do till this very day, fearing they might be called Liberal if they support any Black initiative. Maybe it is our National Black leaders, who continue to broker deals for their own personal gain? If you ask me, it is probably all of the above. Remember one thing, there were a lot of Red States in the last presidential election, and we need thirty eight states to affirm our right to vote again, according to the Voting Rights Act. Wouldn't it be hilarious if Supreme Court Justice Clarence Thomas couldn't vote? Or Secretary of State Condelezza Rice. Man I would die laughing. This Voting Rights Act was passed in the sixties under Lyndon B. Johnson and in the year 2007 we still don't have the right to vote without stipulations. Now whose fault is that? NAACP don't you think something is wrong with that? And if you don't, then something is really wrong with you. And if you do think something is wrong with that, then why the hell hasn't something been done about it after all these years? Forty years! Two generations! You are useless to our people. How can you so called Black National Leaders sit there and let such a travesty continue? You know the more I continue to write, the more I feel the need to do a raw version of this book, to tell it just like it is. Somebody please explain the rationale. What if the Voting Rights Act didn't pass? You Negroes would be marching all over the place screaming bloody murder. But in reality you are the ones who are letting it get to a point where something like that could actually happen. Again, the same thing at Texaco. For generations they sat there, saying nothing. We must begin to realize that we are responsible for our fate. They can't do anything to us that we don't let them do. It's disgraceful how this is allowed to continue and nothing is being done. And if there is something being done, then what the hell is taking so long for something that is our constitutional right. I wonder if King knew that the road was going to be this long and winding? Because if he knew, it is sure difficult to see, with the people we have in these positions of representation, how we will ever make it to the Promise Land, not unless he meant after we were all dead.

Personally, to undertake another battle like Texaco for a bunch of sorry *House Negro*es just ain't happening. Actually, it was my Coach who told me that it was time to stop being like a salmon swimming upstream all the time. I had climbed to the top of the mountain, and I had been to the mountaintop, and now it was time to come down. I guess when you are fighting all the time it is hard to stop. Someone has to coach you down. And that's what mine did for me. Interestingly, my colleague who was part of this project never developed the type of relationship I had with my Coach and eventually failed. That's when I realized how strategic the process was in the selection of my Coach. They were really trying to help me succeed. You know what is even more interesting, the respect I got from the people in the streets that saw the article. I was shocked when I was around the way and several individuals from the hood were saying, "Yo, I saw the article, Yeah Baby!" Honestly, I didn't even think they read the paper, except for who got popped, or shot. I received a lot of positive reinforcement about the article from my people in the streets. I'll never forget one afternoon during lunch break at the Mall, some young teenagers said, "yo, that's the guy, the one in the newspaper." They came up to me and asked if it was me? I smiled and said yes. It was awesome to see such enthusiasm from young people. You may wonder why would that be? It's simple! It's the *House Negro* vs. the *Field Negro* mentality. The *House Negro* is, *massa* "we" sick, vs. the *Field Negro, massa,* hope your ass die. Our young people understand and respect the Field! What is sad is that most of these differences between *house* and *field* occur because of ones' material status. But let me warn you *House Negro*, you keep trusting in your material status, however, when the day comes when *massa* decides to kick you off the plantation, don't come over here looking for sympathy from me. Don't come over here screaming racism. Go to *massa*, cause ain't nobody home! This is a warning to you *House Negro*, change or else, because one way or another you are about to be totally exposed for the useless, self-serving, treacherous, treasonous, inhumane being that you really are. Once I get finished with you, you won't be able to even sell your soul to the devil. I am going to pull the cover off of you like when you expose maggots to light. So run for cover *House Negro*, because soon your blackness is going to be your best friend, actually your only friend. The end is near, but you won't even have the chance to repent!

Chapter 7

Me & My Coach

As I had previously stated, it was the beginning of a beautiful relationship. He was so cool, dressed cool, looked cool, acted cool, everything that I was about. I felt very comfortable in sharing with him the magnitude of the challenge he was really about to undertake in attempting to take me under his wing. I felt it my responsibility to inform him of the collateral damage that I had caused during this war. He was absolutely right. I had pissed off a whole lot of people. I showed him some of the memos to the CEO, and the memos pertaining to the individuals who caught my wrath. I will say this, I did Blacks with the same contempt I did Whites. What's interesting, as I think about certain things in my entire professional career, is that my worst experiences had been under two Black female supervisors, and my worst experience in life was just recently with a Black female judge. This women, I really want to call her a *fuckin bitch*, but I guess I better not, tried to destroy me, more than once. What made it worse, was that she could just sit there in her robe and say and do whatever the *fuck* she wanted as long as that Court Officer was there. She knew there wasn't a damn thing I could do as she proceeded to legally *fuck* me in my ass. It was like having a Colonoscopy without anesthesia. That's another story, however, my point is that these Black females take out whatever personal issues they have with Black men, and use their positions to exact revenge. *Shit*, they are worse than any *massa*, clansmen, or any white enemy we could ever encounter. They are simply just *fucked up*! The one at Texaco left me no alternative but to challenge her evaluation to the fullest extent. I literally had to blow her up. With the other Black female supervisor, I just eventually quit that job, and with the Black female Judge, well, I will just have to leave that up to my God to destroy that you know what!. Can I ask God to destroy that you know what? Maybe not, however, this is the irony and case and point or point and fact of this entire story. Someone from my race was and is trying to destroy me. Before my Black supervisor at Texaco, I at least had good evaluations from my white supervisors. She, however, gave me the worst evaluation ever in my six or seven year history at Texaco. I remember wrestling with whether or not she was gonna catch my wrath. I also thought about the implications of having a poor evaluation in my permanent file. The ramifications could have been devastating. It's because of shit like this! I was like, how is she going to give me a bad review when it was me who had learned and trained the department on a new computerized accounting system? And what was left for me to do but to appeal to the white establishment to override her destructive intentions. May not be so lucky with the judicial branch, cause we all know ain't no real justice for the *poor* Black man in America! I just got my objection back from the Courts, and guess what? I won! Yeah right! I get to go back in front of the same you know what who fucked me in the first place. Yeah, justice my ass. Anyway, our department was about to undergo this accounting transition that was going to affect every department at Headquarters. This system had at least ten thousand vendor codes, a million codes for Internal Auditing and the Comptrollers Department for IRS reporting, you name it. This was how serious the work was at Corporate Headquarters. One mistake in a code or payment could affect an entire audit. You would think that the person responsible for that would be very important in the scheme of things. Everyone in the department was trembling about going on line. I remember the meeting we had in the Conference Center, and listening to my colleagues in the Financial Planning Department panic. I had just come back from the office in Bellaire, Texas for training and had grasped the whole system in two days. So during the panic I decided to raise my hand and explain the basic operational procedures of the system. The whole room was shocked. I guess they didn't believe that a little ole Black boy like me could have already conceptualized this complex accounting procedure, and be ready to train the Financial Planning Group also. What, you think I was at Texaco just because of my good looks? I told you I was pretty smart! Believe it or not, I am actually very smart. I guess it is hard for some people to conceive how someone who doesn't walk around like he is better than his brothers, or associates with the home-boys in Shipping and Receiving or the Mailroom, can be to bright. I guess if I walked around like those other *House Negro*es, then it might have been easier for them to understand. But that's the problem. We think because we may have more education than other Blacks, that we are better than they are. You know what I found even more interesting than that? There were a whole lot of whites at Texaco who weren't college educated either, yet we, meaning those stupid, ignorant *House Negro*es would break their neck to be recognized by them. Why is that? Why do we, meaning those *House Negro*es, feel that in order to be validated they have to be accepted by whites, regardless of the white person's status. Even if they are nothing but 'White Trash.' Is this what that post-traumatic slave syndrome thing is about? Are we really that twisted in the membrane? I guess we are. I became so proficient in COMSET, as the system was referred to, that they would pray for me to make a mistake. It would take two people to correct the reports because you had to be sure that all the vendor codes were correct and all the codes for Internal Auditing were correct for reporting purposes. If any were entered incorrectly, there were a series of steps to reverse the transaction from Internal Auditing. This is just to give you an idea of the complexity involved. All the financials were generated by this system. This was also how all the vendors received payment. I remember one feature, which dealt with the terms of payment, net 30, net 15, etc. that for some vendors I would make sure they were taken care of personally. When I reflect back on the operation at the headquarters of Texaco, everything was serious. One mistake, even in deliveries, would warrant a phone call. And don't let it be from Mahogany Row. That's where the Senior Level Executives played. So here I was faced with this evaluation. Before, I would just sign the document, but this time I decided to review it and really think about what was on this form. Should I have shown favoritism to her because she was Black and about to cut my damn throat? Sorry Charlie, I ain't no sacrificial lamb for no one. I am not going to let anyone look good at my expense. Wasn't built that way. The complaint was that I didn't' put forth enough effort and commitment, my response was that if you gave me something commensurate with my educational level maybe I would. And again, just because the work you give me is complex to you, you can't even begin, and are really not qualified, to evaluate someone with a higher level of education. Sounds kind of arrogant, maybe, but no matter how much experience you may have, until you understand what that level of learning is all about, you cannot begin to understand, that what is challenging to you is effortless for me. Oh boy, now why did I go say that? Not only was my supervisor not college educated, but the manager of the Financial Planning Group was not either. Although they had been there forever, I challenged the fact that work experience does not qualify you as supervisor, but neither does being college educated. I truly believe that a balance of both, work experience and education facilitates that skill set, but one of none and none of the other is what was being bred in Texaco, at least in the services arena. I was determined to make them respect my degree, even if it killed them. They wanted to chain me to my desk, yet I was determined not to be a corporate slave. I got up whenever I wanted to. I came back when I wanted to. They would complain about the amount of invoices to be processed, I would sit down for an hour an do one hundred or more and then they would have to spend the entire day correcting the report for any errors, which were far and few between, but nonetheless, the reports still had to be corrected. It was a tedious process, because there were several codes that were involved and every code had to be checked against the report. They also weren't as proficient in the codes as I had become, so they had to manually check to make sure the codes were correct. All in all, they hated me and I hated them. Personally, I wasn't no damn bean counter anyway. By the way, they still had their regular daily work to complete. Things were sure beginning to get nasty in there. This is one reason why I am such a strong advocate for education. Without my education, I wouldn't have had a leg, foot, ankle, or anything to stand on. With it, I was able to counter any and every attempt to sabotage me. It's like, without education, is like going to war without armor or adequate ammunition. With education you never run out of ammunition. Even though all I wanted to do was play professional basketball, I knew that as long as I had my education I had something to fall back on. It was sort of like my little safety net. I knew I could always find a job as long as I had a degree, and once I got my foot in the door, it was over. I became more and more confident as my work experience increased with my education. Personally, I think I would have done a lot better in New York City. It's just different down there. Without my degree, I would hate to think where I might be at this point in time. Probably the best comparison I can think of especially for those young people debating about education is, it's like jumping out of a plane without a parachute, or if you're gonna fight, make sure you have the proper equipment. You wouldn't get into the ring without a mouthpiece unless you want your teeth knocked out. Same difference, if you're gonna get in the ring with these guys, you have to be prepared, because they will knock your teeth out of your mouth and down your throat. So after all this fighting going on, you can begin to see that Me and My Coach had a lot of work to do. Personally, I didn't know how the hell we were supposed to fix this. Interestingly enough, as I became more mainstream in the company, so to speak, the *House Negro*es were less intimidated exchanging dialogue with me publicly. And as different doors began to open, and I was beginning to shine, everyone wanted to know how I got this opportunity. I remember one gentleman I used to jog with inadvertently mentioned this program with Texaco where the chosen few Blacks would go speak to High School students. After realizing it slipped out and I said I would love to do that, I became involved in the program called AMBYESE: Annual Minority Business Youth Embarkment Services. A star was born. The kids loved me. What was interesting was that this program had been going on for several years, yet I had never been introduced to it. Now why do you think that was? Simple, as far as the chosen few Blacks were concerned, I was not good enough to participate in the circles they were in. They figured that since I delivered boxes I wasn't good enough to speak to those students. I guess now that I was in Financial Planning I was a bit more prestigious and acceptable. But the whole thing should have been about teaching the importance of education to our youth. Come to find out, the gentleman who I used to jog with didn't have a degree, yet he was in charge of the program. I wonder what he was telling them, since he didn't have a degree? Anyway, for the next few years I became part of that group that went to speak to the High School students. These are the kinds of things that upset me with those sorry *House Negro*es. Simply because they had no idea who I was or what I was about, they categorized me as unacceptable. Just because I didn't come with a rubber stamp of approval or some predetermined title from the white man, I was nobody. But these were the same ones who, during the lawsuit, sat on the sidelines and watched. That same person who inadvertently told me about the program was actually the poster boy for Texaco during the settlement. Afterwards when the rightsizing was going down and his position was being threatened, he was talking some garbage about, if they mess with him he's going to tell all. I just looked at him and said, 'I hear you.' But what he didn't know was that there wasn't anybody home, and nobody cared anymore, and the cameras were gone. Actually, he eventually got fired anyway. They paraded him around during the press conference. You know how there is always one of us in the picture. Wouldn't want to upset those dignified *House Negro*es. We couldn't have that, now could we. It's a shame how easily we are pacified. It's interesting how when I delivered boxes the *House Negro*es didn't hesitate to ask me to play basketball. When I previously did that psychological comparative analysis of how we interact with each other vs. say Hispanics, it totally intrigues me that when we see each other we barely speak. I'm telling you, I have seen it and experienced it for myself. Then there are Black women who, when they see me in the gym, won't even look in my direction until they see that the white people at the gym think I'm a god, then it's Ok to speak to me. I still need to be validated by whites before these wanna be *bourgeois bitches* speak to me. Why is that? I don't know, but it's sad. These are the things that I am trying to bring to the forefront so we can really start to look at how we interact with each other. However, let me be in the streets with a suit on, then they are ready to speak in a minute. Personally, I hate that. Then you wonder why rappers talk so negatively about Black women. Some of it is justified, because they really do things that are basically equivalent to a prostitute. We must take a real good look in the mirror as to why things are the way they are between our Black women and the Black man. Maybe it's because of the things we do to ourselves. How can we make any real progress if I as a Black man can't get any respect from a Black woman unless I have on a suit, or driving a fancy car? What garbage. Take a look at our athletes and all of our entertainers. Although some of them are rich, ain't none of them wealthy. We don't own any teams in any sport. We don't own any TV or MGM's or Turner Broadcasting Networks. We don't own any Stadiums, Coliseums, Convention Centers, even with all that money these individuals make. That is the key word, individuals. Individually we are fine, we are the leading consumers in America and probably the world, but we still don't own a damn thing. When I look at rap videos, I say that someone needs to own a vineyard somewhere that makes Krystal, or Champagne, when you consider all the alcohol they consume, or a diamond or gold mine in South Africa with all the platinum, diamonds and gold they be sporting. I remember writing this rap titled "time to represent", it started out by saying, we're making everyone rich and ain't respected. No one was interested in hearing that. They would tell me that's old school. But shooting up each other and selling drugs was selling everywhere. One must first understand who controls what sells. We only can produce what the people who own the recording labels feel will sell. So when we are calling our women bitches and hoes, we basically are selling what the people who are the producers want out there. If they do not sign off on the record deals for that type of music it wouldn't be in existence, but nobody wants to talk about that. So here I am walking around with all this philosophical socio-economic mumbo jumbo, wanting to find a way to help society. To change the way we as Blacks treat each other and begin to approach this life in America with a different mentality. Personally, if we keep going the way we are, I really worry about what the future is going to look like for my daughter. I worry even more, now that I have a son. So as my Coach made me realize that the war was over and it was time to take care of me and mine, somewhere in the back of my mind, I couldn't help but think that economically, we spend billions a year and are no further than we were two generations ago. How could that possibly be? I conclude, we had real leaders back then. See, you must understand how important leadership is in the equation of everything. An organization is only as good as its leadership. A country is only as good as its leadership. A sports franchise is only as good as its leadership. And we Black people are only as good as our leadership! So, I guess if we aren't any further than we were two generations ago then one could easily and logically deduce that our leadership ain't worth much of anything. As you can probably deduce, I have been walking around with this stuff for a while. And as much as my Coach tried to help me, these areas of concern were always going to be on my mind. However, he did teach me how to be smarter about how I did things. As a matter of fact, he taught me so much that I became a pro. Going to work was fun, but he warned me not to lose that fire. In other words, don't get too comfortable around these folks, cause their memory is like an elephant, and they ain't about to forget all the trouble you caused them. One other point I want to make, especially to those misguided *House Negro*es. Remember when rap was like poison, and rappers were the scum of the earth, that's until M&M, the white rapper came on the seen. Hell, they were ready to label him the 'king of rap'. Now everywhere you go rappers are there, performing in places and at events they never were accepted at. Sort of like when segregation was the way of life in the south. Those *House Negro*es who were condemning rap, now that it became socially acceptable to whites, it's alright to clap to the beat. I hope when Christ comes back he sends all of you pathetic, hypocritical *House Negro*es straight to hell, because that is where you really belong. You can't stand up for anything until *massa* says it's Ok. Oh yeah, now there's Christian rap. Don't know much about it but, I remember when Kirk Franklin first came out with the funky rap beat in Christian music, those *House* Christians were bout to lose their minds. Personally, I like Yolanda Adams, but I enjoy when those traditionalists get shook up a bit and don't know what to do. That's how misguided we are. Why is it that we can't take a stance on something unless validation comes from them, meaning whites? My colleague used to always say to me that if you don't stand for something you'll fall for everything. Personally, before I took that stance against Texaco, my life had been mediocre at best. At least now I am writing a book. I would have never imagined that in my life I would be doing this or suing a company like Texaco. This is probably the most important project to date in my life. There are still obstacles and challenges, however, isn't that what life is all about? We need to embrace ourselves, and it seems to be problematic for us to do so unless someone else validates it for us first. That's a real problem. That is the problem. You know, every time I begin to analyze, or logically deduce, or attempt to theorize, to maybe understand the how's and the why's of this all, the thoughts, from my mind, to the pen in my hand, to the paper always comes back to those *House Negro*es. When you look back in time to the origins of slavery, like it or not, it was us who sold us. And we are still selling ourselves. Selling out, that is. Selling our souls. I can at least say with conviction that the road I may have traveled was rough, but I never sold out. My soul is still mine. My life and alleged career could have been different in Corporate America, but personally I never wanted to be in Corporate America. I always felt as though it was some type of modernized plantation for modernized slaves. I will leave you with this one thought my people that I hope will resound for generations. Get educated! Not just for the possibility of a decent job, but because you need to be able to see and understand what is going on in the world around you. It is the only avenue available for real progress. I'll tell you a little secret. If you see white people doing it, believe me there is a reason why. They don't do anything for nothing. And they don't give anything for nothing. There is always something that is for their benefit and personal gain at the end of it all. Today I see more old white men in the gym than ever. Then you wonder why they live longer than us. White women live in the gym, and now Hispanics are in the gym like never before. You would think with the cost of health care we would be trying to take better care of ourselves. But I don't see any of the elder Black males in the gym. I hardly see Black women in the gym to the degree I see Whites and Hispanics. Where are we? We need to reevaluate what is important. Health should be one of our main priorities. This is why we succumb to so many diseases. This is why we die earlier than our counterparts. There was a time our physical superiority used to be our pride. After a few drug epidemics in our communities, we have been broken. So what now? What's the plan? Let me explain how leadership makes all the difference in the world. For example, just analyzing the process my colleague and myself went through. He was already in the program. I didn't get in until after the article ran. So you can see that my entry was hostile, so to speak. The reason I excelled and he didn't wasn't because of anything special I did. It wasn't because I was a college graduate and he wasn't. That had nothing at all to do with it. It was the Coaches we had that made the difference. Even though he was selected to be in the program, his coach, whom I had met once, never was around to formulate any type of strategy for him. Mine would give me instructions, call me to check and see if I had done as I was instructed and would come to Headquarters to hang out with me for the day and see where I was with everything he had instructed me to complete. My Coach would say, "Pete, I want you to do XYZ." I would be, "come on, you have got to be kidding yo!" "Just do it!" You see, if he wasn't compatible with me and if I perceived him as one of those misguided *House Negro*es, there wouldn't have been anything he could have said that meant anything to me. However, he was someone who I could identify with, and truly respected. They knew I would listen to him. Why they selected someone that they knew I would listen to and possibly achieve the desired results of this program is a mystery to me. But the person responsible for the selection of him as my Coach was the former EEOC, and you know how I felt about him and he about me. That also turned out to be a really good story. A lot of good stories were beginning to emerge with Me and My Coach. After he saw all the people I had attempted to destroy, one of the first

121

assignments he gave me was to make nice with my Black female supervisor. He said he had spoken with her and she said I spent too much time on the phone. I said it was business most of the time. He said, "I bet you look like you are having fun." I told him, I had great relationships with the vendors and the customers. He said "Look, when you are on the phone, whether it is personal or professional, always make it look like it is business." I was like, "damn that's sweet." He also told me to organize my work area differently. Not that there was anything wrong with it, just change the perception of it. Keep a journal, so when anyone walks by they'll be wondering what the hell is he doing? What in the world is he writing now? And remember, "be nice to your Black female supervisor." I was like, "come on man." He was like, "Pete!" I changed my style just a little. While I was on the phone I was always professional even during personal phone calls. I sat at my desk more, but did less work, but everyone was happy. I was the new model citizen or corporate employee model. The Black female supervisor was so pleased that she went back to my Coach and said, "I don't know what you said to him, but thank you!" My Coach came back to me saying "yes Pete!" I thought my work was done. Then he came back to me and said, "I want you to make nice with your supervisor's boss." I was like, "you have got to be kidding me!" She was hard and she was tough and she never smiled. She just walked around like a tyrant or something. Again, we went through our Pete, Ok, Ok! How was I supposed to do this. See that's what I mean. He would tell me to do something and if I was not sure, he would tell me where to start. He was mentoring me, and grooming me to be successful. So he said, "just start out by saying good morning." I was like, "OK, I can do that." My colleague's coach was nowhere to be found. One can only begin to imagine what things might have been like if I had a different coach. Scary isn't it. I probably would have gotten fired from Texaco and would have been blacklisted from the corporations in Westchester. Heaven only knows where else. One must remember that Texaco was an international company, and this lawsuit had put them in a spotlight they didn't want or need. This could have been a very different story. It easily could have been 'the war continues'. Considering I didn't and still don't like people telling me what to do, I guess this book better be a success. However, Me and My Coach were becoming quite a team. He would call me and say I'm flying in from Pittsburgh on such and such a day, and we're going to have lunch and spend the day together, off site of course. We actually had a lot of nice lunches and strategic sessions together. Our main refuge was the Doral Arrowwood Country Club. We would frequent there often, on Texaco, of course. We were having a ball, to be perfectly honest. He would give me a new strategic plan, and then we would sit there and he would tell me how he was planning to retire and go on the Pro Senior Golf Tour. We would laugh for hours as he used to confide in me how Texaco had no idea what to do with a Black man like me. He also shared with me why he left Corporate America and started his own consulting business. It's basically the same old story. He was with this firm and when it came time to make him a partner, they balked. Oh not right now, maybe in a few more years. "Same shit different day." Believe it or not, because I sure didn't, my supervisor's boss and I had developed a very good professional rapport. Once again, my Coach came back very pleased. Word was really starting to spread. Things were going so well no one would have ever believed. For example, I had to do something or go somewhere and missed the departmental Christmas party. Next thing I knew, the Head of the Department, who I basically had called a racist, his second in command and my supervisor's boss took me out for a special luncheon to make up for me missing the party. Imagine that! But that was how great things were going. They actually took me out to say thank you for the tremendous turnaround. It probably was because I stopped raising pure unadulterated hell. For the most part, I really hadn't changed all that much. I was just following the advice my Coach was giving to me and it was working. They were loving me as much as they could love me. It was a good feeling to be in the mainstream so to speak, after swimming so long upstream, fighting this inherently, systemically, racist corporate culture. It really came down to respect. But then again, personally, they never disrespected me. Professionally, they may have insulted my intelligence, however, I am not sure if that was intentional or just part of the culture fostered by those who sat around never voicing any discontentment. I just can't understand how someone can sit there and not say anything if they are being disrespected. I mean, I was not personally being disrespected, but I guess after I learned the system and how it was designed, I was outraged. Maybe they didn't know the system. But how can you sit there for all those years and not be aware of a system that is oppressing you? I am trying to find some rationalization for the justification of those who would sit there. I wish there was someone who could help me understand it. I am trying to have compassion for these people. They have cost our race so much and have made it much more difficult for our progress. I guess I need to thank God for the ones who weren't afraid to leave the plantation. But look at where we are today. Where are we? Maybe this was the new kinder gentler Pete emerging. I guarantee that won't last but for so long before I get angry again and be ready to call a spade a spade and a *House Negro* a *House Negro*. Yeah here we go! Thankfully, my Coach kept me focused, and my infant daughter kept me smiling, truly a gift from God. I know I said this before, but I remember after that article ran and the implications of even agreeing to do it, the scrutiny, and how Texaco tried to stop the press on it, when I think about the sacrifice that a few of us made and those bastards calling everyday about the money, simply disgusts me. The risk I took was tremendous, but I took it anyway because it needed to be brought out into the open. I guess in hindsight I can say it was liberating. If there was anything that I could say or would say to those useless *House Negro*es, I would say that it is liberating to express yourself and stand up for yourself. I was never the same after the lawsuit. It was probably the lawsuit that gave me the courage to stand up and not take any more of the bullshit. I wasn't having it, and that made me even more dangerous. You can bargain all you want, but there comes a time when you have to stand up and say enough is enough and I ain't taking it no more. It was for that reason and for that reason alone that things became different for me. If I had just been satisfied with that little bit of money, I would have been sitting there with no purpose, just collecting a paycheck. I mean, I needed to get paid but if I never would have said anything or never went to the internal investigation, what little bit of future I had would not have ever begun. As I said, things were really going well and somewhere along the line I had received two promotions. I was like yeah! We're really making progress now. This is the way it should have always been. My Coach told me to send thank you cards, and I really thought it inappropriate, but he was my Coach and I was following his instructions. Let me tell you, I had people damn near ready to cry. Man, my Coach was amazing. He was always pointing me in a new direction that was taking me higher and higher. In the interim I decided on my own to send a memo to the former EEOC and let him know that I really appreciated what he did in the selection process of my Coach. Because when I think about the hell I caused him, he probably should have given me the coach my colleague had who was never around and didn't do a damn thing for him. His coach left him hanging high and dry. He didn't, but he could have, and if he reads this book, I think it is only right for him to know that I really appreciated the care that went into selecting my Coach. Later I came to find out that he and my Coach were actually friends. Interesting how this circle works. I ran into him in the cafeteria one day and he said that he was hearing nothing but good things about me. I said thanks, and he replied "don't thank me, it's you that's doing the work. You're the one that's making it happen." Yeah I was, but then again, I wasn't even considered initially for this program. Just goes to show, I could have been doing all the very same things, but without the green light from the CEO this would have never happened. And it wasn't so much of a green light vs. here's your chance, and if you blow this your ass is dead meat! That's more what it was like. But I wasn't afraid of none of them. And as far as I was concerned I was going to get down like I do. I was smart and I knew it, and I was going to show just how smart this little "black jelly bean" was. I was not gonna give them a damn excuse to say oh, he failed. No ammunition from me baby! Trust me, this could have gone the other way just like it did for my boy. I just said, give me the ball and watch me do my thing. I also was smart enough to know that this wasn't happening just because of me. No matter how egotistical I may sound, I ain't stupid. But I was walking around Texaco like I was king. Occasionally, I would run into the CEO in my travels through the halls of Texaco or on the elevator, and I know in the back of his mind he may have been calling me god knows what, especially since I always addressed him by his first name. Ironically, we had the same first name. He was probably saying, how dare this punk address me by my first name. Who the hell does he think he is? But he would always respond back and sometimes even address me first. Pete, I would reply back Pete. And that's how it was. One thing I did learn in Texaco was, if, if you were even the slightest bit intimidated by these people, you would not survive. People would tremble with fear at the sound of the CEO's name. He ruled Texaco like the Pharaohs ruled Egypt. I am serious. I am telling you that when you look at it, there wasn't much difference being in the streets than it was in the confines of corporate. That is why I always used to tell people that 'the CEO was the warden but I ran the prison'. I remember at the last picnic I went to at Texaco, I wore this black fitted dress muscle shirt. My biceps were bulging, my abs were ripped, my chest was enormous, I was probably in the best shape ever. The girls were like, "damn Pete! It's like that!" I just smiled. I remember standing, talking to one of my homeboys and the CEO came walking by all hard like he was not gonna acknowledge we were standing there. Then he looked up and damn near had cardiac arrest. He was like, Oh Shit! As he reached out to shake the 'King' of the prison's hand. You really had to be there, it was very, very intriguing to say the least. My boy, who is also from around the way, saw this and started dying laughing. He was like, "Oooooh, Pete, did you see that?" I was like, nonchalantly, "yeah I saw it." He said, "you're a bad man." I said, "I told you I run the prison and he is just the warden." Yeah, things were moving right along. It was like a prison, so to speak, when you look at it somewhat in the abstract. You take a break when you are told, you have to always let someone know where you are going and tell someone when you're going to the bathroom. I mean, there is professional courtesy, but some people were on lockdown, I was never locked down. And now, I was able to do whatever I wanted within the professional boundaries that I had come to master so well with the help of my Coach. I could have become a real SOB, but I chose to respect my colleagues, and always maintain my professional integrity. Yep, things were going well and I was about to begin my new assignment. It is amazing what can be done in a corporation such as Texaco. They can erase all their systemic racial practices whenever they get ready. Just goes to show you that it is not their intention to do so. That's what's so sad and disheartening about the whole thing. On the other hand, if more of us would stand up and speak out, maybe, just maybe, things would be a whole hell of a lot different. I knew a man who said "by any means necessary", everyone thought he was anti establishment, anti white. To the contraire, he just was speaking out against the racial injustices afflicting his race. He also knew that in order to get the powers that be to change, you have to make them change, given their inherent propensity towards oppression and violence. Sometimes that is exactly what it takes. Sometimes you will have to fight fire with fire. I remember, as I attempted to try it the civilized way, going through the EEOC and writing to my Department Head, expressing my concerns about my future at Texaco. That approach yielded nothing. It wasn't until I was mad as hell with these bastards, and ready to go ballistic that any change occurred. Personally, I believe in non-violence but you have to admit, when you look back at the non-violent movements, and the brutality that was inflicted upon our people, you have to wonder why in the world would anyone take such a position. I guess I am grateful they did because God only knows what type of society we would be living in at this present time if they had not taken that approach. I think those *House Negroes* who have benefited from the bloodshed of our forefathers need to wake up and realize that they wouldn't be anywhere if it weren't for those sacrifices. The other side of this history is the race of people who did this to our people. How barbaric, uncivilized, and ignorant! Just because a people wanted equality, a people wanted freedom, a people wanted truth, justice and the American way. You mean to tell me that just because we wanted to be treated like humans, we went through all of that abuse? When they look back on this so-called "great society," and when the truth be told, God help us and forgive us all. But like I said, companies like Texaco had the power to change all of that, why they don't is another story, but I watched how they could do anything they wanted and my new assignment was living proof. I should have never even had to go through these changes. That should have been part of the employment process, to identify and develop its employees where they would excel. The interesting part to these trials and tribulations is that Texaco didn't even do that for their white employees. But at least the salary differential wasn't a factor. They basically abused everyone, and if you didn't like it, leave. The old 'be thankful you have a job' scenario was the unwritten rule of thumb. However, they paid their white employees at a much higher rate than their black employees doing the same job, and that is what was going to be one of the key areas if the case would have gone to trial. The differential was staggering. It was like seventy some odd million dollars in salary differentiation between whites and blacks. I guess that was one way to make sure they kept us out of their neighborhoods. And for those *House Negro*es to act like they didn't know was just as disgusting. I don't think I would have joined this lawsuit if I knew now what I thought I knew then. Yes I would have. I was so pissed after they tried to play me for stupid, all I wanted to do was let them know that this Negro ain't stupid. I am going to be your worst nightmare. And I was heading right in that direction. Why do you think everyone was so pleased after Me and My Coach started working together? I was giving them hell. Maybe they sent him to calm me down. He certainly did just that, but we were having a ball at the same time. When I told him about my new assignment he already knew and he was proud of me. He looked good, I looked good and Texaco looked good. It was win, win all across the board, who could ask for anything more.

Chapter 8

My New Assignment

Next thing I knew, I was being shipped upstairs to the Community Relations Department, part of my fast track in the new Texaco organization. I remember being told that I have to meet with this gentleman who was the Director of the department. I heard about him, and I was like, here we go again, another one of those newcomers who everyone thinks is great. I really didn't feel like meeting him, but I really didn't have a choice in the matter. Things were running relatively effortlessly in my department. Eventually, I went up to meet with him, and boy oh boy it wasn't hard to tell why Texaco chose him as Director. Here was this damn near white looking African American with the black wavy hair trying to act like he was so sophisticated and the new sheriff for Texaco. He didn't know who he was about to encounter, but I played it cool. He asked me questions and I gave all the right answers and, of course, he said I had to meet with his superior. Of course he wanted to know about the lawsuit and what really happened. I sidestepped that land mine and basically said some executives got caught on tape saying some real ugly things about African Americans. I switched it to him to find out where he came from and how he ended up at Texaco. He shared with me and I thought that was pretty cool. Prior to his arrival, he was at another corporation and basically had run into a brick wall. The new Head of the Department used to be at that same organization and arranged for him to get the position. I know that Texaco was real comfortable with him because he looked just like them. I mean, you could tell that he was not white, but you knew that Texaco chose him for just that reason. You know, it's like that Willie Lynch theory. Put the light skin *niggas* in charge or against the darker ones. This was used effectively in South Africa Apartheid. The lighter Negroes were treated better than the darker ones, and even though it was not much better, when apartheid was being abolished, the lighter ones were afraid they would lose their slightly favored status over the darker Africans. How pathetic is that? Actually it's an outright disgrace to our race. It is that same mentality instilled in the *House Negro* that leaves us in the pitiful condition we are in today. I mean, look at Apartheid and the brutality of that system, and because one group was afforded preferential treatment, they didn't want to see justice prevail, ending that brutal system, even though both groups were being oppressed by this system. They could not even appreciate the ending of Apartheid due to their preferential treatment under this oppressive system. Never mind that thousands upon thousands were suffering and killed because of this racist system. Never mind that people were fighting and dying to be free from this system of oppression. This is why we need to purge our race of these people. I doubt if any of those light skinned *niggas even* voted for Nelson Mandela. How can they look themselves in the mirror knowing they were for the continuation of such a brutal system to humanity? They really need to go to hell. They are the useless scum of the earth. At least you knew why the whites wanted it to remain. But how could anyone of color who knew what this system stood for, validate standing up for it? I'm telling you, as long as we continue down this path of destruction, the enemy doesn't even have to worry about us. It's a sorry tale of a group of people who think because they have slightly more than those less fortunate that they are not also victimized. Heaven help us. What a bunch of ignorant fools. All their light skin is, is a reflection of the rape and sexual deviancy of their captors, and over here, *massa* creeping into the slave quarters late at night while he thought his wife was sleeping. Till this day we are still unable to comprehend this divisive ploy.

So there we were, him and me, the Negro who would rather apartheid continue because of his favored status, and the Negro who wanted nothing more than to destroy it. No, it wasn't all that, because too many times those who are really against racism and all its elements are light skinned, because they do know why and how their pigmentation became compromised. Overall, his credentials were impeccable, yet, he also had been victimized by the glass ceiling of Corporate America. The difference was that I realized why I was going through what I was going through. Then again, there was a time when I too was clueless. I guess we continue to believe that one day we will be judged according to our merit, and not the color of our skin. Maybe it's that equal opportunity employer that is part of the requirement on an employment application. I remember I was sounding like I was doing the interview, determining if he really was a suitable employee. I realized that there were some areas he just couldn't understand, and because of his background, it left him clueless. But that wasn't his fault. Again, it goes back to that Willie Lynch Theory. I know there were some things he never would experience, because he made an excellent poster boy. That wasn't his fault either. It was the culture we were in, the nature of the beast. Shortly after our interview, I met with the Head of the Texaco Foundation, which the Community Relations Department came under. She, too, wanted to know what happened inside Texaco. I diplomatically explained that there were some differences but myself and Texaco made up and I am now being afforded an opportunity to develop and prove myself a valuable asset to the company. You know, all that talk they like to hear. Next thing you know, I was in. They were trying to figure out where they were going to place me. A two-window office was available and I was slotted to take it over, but remember what I told you about offices? Someone raised holy hell about it. Next thing you knew I was in a cubicle. I smiled because I knew what had happened. They didn't know, because both of them were new to the organization. My Coach had this saying, that 'the more things changed the more they stayed the same'. Man was he ever right. So my new assignment had begun. I was going out with the Head of the Community Relations Department to meet with members of the community to convince people of the new direction Texaco was undertaking, and identify organizations we wanted to donate money to. It was very interesting to say the least. It was obvious we had different ideas of who we wanted to donate money to.

He wanted to donate money to organizations that were already established and didn't have any real challenges. I remember one organization where we went to meet the Executive Director, who was formerly from the private sector, that had numerous connections with his former acquaintances in the business world. They didn't need any help from Texaco. On the way back to the office he says to me, now that's the type of organization Texaco is looking to partner with. I was like, here we go, another misdirected *House Negro*. Sure it would make him look good and Texaco look good, but I was more concerned about organizations like the Boys and Girls Club and the YMCA, in the disenfranchised areas. What about them? They are the ones who really need help from an organization like Texaco. Basically his response was, "We don't want to get involved with organizations that are really going to need us. We want to partner with organizations that will be able to maintain themselves after we assist them." He was basically explaining to me how this game of Corporate giving goes. My thing was, you give millions to the Metropolitan Opera every year. What about Alvin Aley, Boys Choir of Harlem? Yeah they would give them some miniscule amount of money, and place all kinds of demands and restrictions on them, and make them jump through hoops like monkeys, but that was how the game was played. I guess you may be beginning to wonder how I was doing in this new assignment. Well after I realized it wasn't really about helping anybody for real, and truly realized it after I set up a meeting with the Mayor in my Community, I guess I was doing just fine. We sat down and were having a discussion about what role Texaco wanted to play in the Community. After listening to all the things that Texaco couldn't do, I was wondering why the hell were we wasting the precious time of the Mayor. Hell, I set this meeting up because I knew that we could do some real good in the Community. That's when I knew that this new imagine of Texaco in the African American Community was bullshit! One afternoon after meeting with the Hispanic Chamber of Commerce, we were scheduled to meet with this Black female politician from Yonkers for lunch, at this upscale restaurant on the Hudson River. My job was to watch and learn how things were done in Community Relations. And that's exactly what I did. I watched my man pull out all these brochures, begin that whole cosmetic, rehearsed script, and then went on to invite this politician to speak at some major event for Texaco reinforcing the Texaco commitment to the African American Community, in other words to those misguided *House Negro*es. She looked at the brochures and basically threw them right back in his face. She then went on to tell him "you must be out of your damn mind, if you think that I would speak at anything you were having. That would be like committing political suicide. Hell, everyone I know who has submitted an application for any monies from Texaco has either been turned down or outright ignored." Then she went on to ask about the person who Texaco brought up from the Houston office who was supposed to be in charge of this special program. Yeah, that special assistant to the CEO, the one all those misguided

House Negroes were applauding about. I told you that it was a bogus
position. She was like, "I can't even get a call back from him."
Homeboy was speechless. Then she asked, "How long have you been
with the company?" He humbly replied about six months if that.
Good thing lunch was about to be served, because homeboy was
definitely about to be eaten alive. Then she looked at me, like, and
who the hell are you? You know I was laughing my head off at my
role model. I smiled and introduced myself, and then the question
that put me in the driver's seat came. "So, how long have you been
with the company?" I coolly replied, "a little over ten years." "Oh
really!" She replied surprisingly. "So you really know what's going
on!" She then asked if I was part of the lawsuit, and I told her I gave
a deposition against Texaco. Next thing you know we were having
this private kind of dialogue. Homeboy couldn't understand what the
hell just happened. The poster boy was shot down and I was soaring
like an eagle. How could that be? I'll tell you! There are some real
Black people out there and Black females who are really concerned
about the future of Black people. Growing up in the 'projects' really
gave me an edge in that meeting. Plus the fact that I was an educated
Black man, whose identity was still intact, made me as lethal as a
double edge sword. A lot of Black people choose to disassociate
from the negative experiences of their past, especially if they were
economically disadvantaged. They spend so much of their time
trying to be accepted and included with the establishment and the
bourgeois. Those are the *House Negro*es who are so misguided, that

they don't know if they are Black or Colored. The first thing they want to do is to move out of the neighborhood. I guess that is why I take so much pride in being able to walk the streets of my old neighborhood and still be respected. I can walk the streets of Harlem and still, the *real* people recognize that I am a part of them and I am not ashamed that they are my brother or sister. I am not ashamed of the plight my people are going through because I know that it could have easily been me, and still can be. If life deals me a terrible blow and I find myself back in the old neighborhood, all I would sing is Welcome Back Carter. My dream was to never be out, but to do something to make it better for the children coming up out of there. Actually I have moved back to *the hood* and it has been very refreshing! The streets can be unforgiving and once they get their hands on you, you may be caught up for life. I've seen it first hand. Individuals with tremendous potential get caught up in the mix of the streets. My saving grace besides God, was my education. I knew that I could always get a job. It might not have been what I wanted, but I could always find a job. That is why I will stress education till I die. It is the key, the gateway out of poverty and most of all, the gateway out of mental slavery. It was obvious she had respect for the person I was, who took a stance against the Corporate Beast. I was beginning to see the significance in what I did. I felt I was officially a real "Black Man". As we continued to conversate, it was refreshing to be able to really share the dynamics with someone who was on the same page and talk about what really happened, and was still happening at

Texaco. Even if she doesn't remember that day, surely I will never forget it. I had a tremendous respect for her after that meeting and it let me know that there were people still fighting for justice for our people. See, I don't hate all Black women, just the fucked up ones, which just happens to be a majority of them. It didn't surprise me when I recently saw her name as a candidate for the Senate. With people like her running for office, maybe there is still hope for Blacks in the future. We had a few more meetings with politicians but the script was always the same. Once we met with a County Legislator who was trying to get this young man a summer job at Texaco. His basic approach was that this young man comes from a disadvantaged background, not from any of these famous named programs that Texaco recruits from. He basically was challenging Texaco to give an opportunity to someone who really needs it, a point that seemed to be missing in the grand scheme of this entire program that Texaco was promoting to improve its relationship within the African American community. I don't know of anyone who benefited from this so-called "New Texaco", except for those *House Negro*es who got positions for doing Texaco's bidding. I was really beginning to wonder how homeboy couldn't see any of this. All he was concerned about was doing exactly what and how he was instructed to operate, I guess. I wonder if it bothered him that he was clueless, or were they paying him enough money not to realize? Reflecting on it all, I guess this was an opportunity for him that he couldn't attain at the previous corporation. So he continued to do Texaco's bidding, even if it wasn't worth the ink the brochures were printed on. I'll never forget this one gentleman, who was in charge of a local independent newspaper in the community. It was called the County Press and the owner was not for sale. He gave Texaco fits. He was exposing this whole charade for what it was. I remember when we had a meeting with this gentleman, he was dead serious, not playing around at all. He was telling it just like it was. He was not impressed like those misguided Negroes who thought that things were great because Texaco appointed this puppet to spearhead a bogus program. Homeboy would ask me, "Why does he hate us so much?" It reminded me of *massa* we sick! He really didn't have a clue, even though he was stuck in a dead-end position at the last corporation. I was beginning to feel sorry for him. He was out of his league with this. I felt comfortable in these situations because I knew I didn't sell out. I was glad to let people know that I was part of this Class Action. I was really beginning to realize that what I did was of real significance. I was feeling like a proud Black Man. I fought the beast, and won. I was beginning to realize as I continued in this capacity, that there were people out there who were dedicated to fighting racial injustice to African Americans, even for those brain dead *House Negro*es. There were people out there still dedicated to trying to keep the '*Dream*' alive, while other Blacks who attained favor because of the *Dream* were busy selling their souls to maintain their favor, denying the sacrifices made in the name of the *Dream*. Personally, I had lost a lot of faith in our leadership, until I realized at the local level, the fight was still alive. It was refreshing to know that there were those who understood that after the cameras were gone and Texaco was no longer in the front page of the news, that there was still a lot that needed to be done. You know shortly after, those meetings with political leaders and such, things came to an abrupt end. I don't believe that it was personal, but the people we went to speak to always wanted to speak to me. They would always want to talk with me because I was there when it all went down. Homeboy was just a benefactor, because. Texaco would have never hired him in a position like that if it weren't for the lawsuit. You have to remember that there was not one, that's right, not one person of color in the entire Corporate Headquarters in a managerial position. Over two thousand employees were at the Headquarters. It's still unbelievable, as I sit here and write this story. It wasn't like this was the sixties, it was almost the year two thousand, the twenty first century, the new millennium. It's disgraceful, that from the sixties almost to the year two thousand, those Blacks employed there did nothing, oh, I mean those classified as *other*, since they made up the majority of people of color. I am telling you here and now and will continue to say it, they are just as much to blame as Texaco. Even more so, because of the negative impact it has had upon our race. Let's face it. We did not get to where we are today because they gave it to us. We had to fight for every damn dime, and for those complacent Negroes to sit there like thank you *massa* for letting me work on this beautiful plantation mentality, it destroyed everything that those who fought and died for, created. If that is not detrimental to a race then I don't know what is. Personally, I was glad I wasn't going to anymore of those meetings because I was tired of being around him. I did meet with the gentleman from the independent newspaper again with their breakfast club. I became less and less impressed with homeboy and I think that he was beginning to sense that. Personally, I had a better command of how things were supposed to really work. As my assignment continued, he kind of put some distance between us with one of the long-term employees of the department. I still had to report to him, so to speak, but I didn't see him that much afterwards. That really was fine with me. The woman I was assigned to probably should have been the one in charge of Community Relations. She knew everyone. She had a real feel for the people who needed Texaco's corporate support. Believe it or not, she was a white female, and we accomplished much together. She would invite me to events that would give me the exposure to the players in the communities. Sometimes that worked two ways. When they would find out I wasn't some employee with a big title at Texaco, the conversation would inevitably always change. I still enjoyed playing that role. I would throw on a tuxedo, and off I would go. I guess I was crossing over. But the more I crossed-over, so to speak, I couldn't wait to get back to the other side. The other side didn't necessarily mean coming out of my tux, it just meant getting away from those fake pretentious *House Negro*es. You should have seen them, all wanting to know where I worked and what kind of work I did. When I would say the Corporate Headquarters of Texaco Inc., they would want to know more about me. Then the next question would be what kind of work do you do? I would reply I am in the Financial Planning Group, on special assignment in Community Relations. Sounds impressive huh? Imagine if I told them I delivered supplies at the Corporate Headquarters. What do you think the response would have been? I'll tell you if you don't know. It would have been what the hell is this peasant doing at this affair. I guess that's what's the sad part of it all. It is those same individuals that proclaim themselves to be Christians, who are perpetrating this travesty. I used to wonder why Christ came riding on a donkey, when he could have come on a chariot or stretch limo, if you get my point. But because he knew the nature of the people, that if he came riding in with all the bling-bling, as they say around the way, all the hypocrites would follow him, proclaiming him king. By riding in on a donkey, he was able to see who really was about his teaching. These people only wanted to know who I was because they saw me in a tuxedo. I looked like someone who they felt comfortable associating with on the surface. I looked like one of them. Actually I looked better than all of them. I have always taken great pride that I am nothing like them. I would rather die first. Matter of fact, if the day ever comes, even after I put together this best seller, if I become anything like them, please put me out of my misery. Personally, I will always advocate for the children and the less fortunate, because it could have easily been me. And I will never forget. I guess I am

144

supposed to pick a charity and all that, when I become rich and famous. But you know what, after all the exorbitant administrative salaries I've seen incurred by these charities, I think I will try a different venue to help those in need. I don't trust a lot of these Not for Profit organizations, with money for the people. I watched the money that Texaco gave to many organizations, and I still have many questions as to how the money was spent to help the ones who it was designated for. I always wondered how athletes and entertainers choose their friends and acquaintances. I mean, how many people really like them for them, and would the same people be around if they didn't have the money? Obviously the answer is no, because they wouldn't be able to get into half the places they choose to frequent. However, I do wonder if they ever stop to think about the what-ifs, and if it's because of the money? Does she really love me? That is why I am always curious, especially when Black male athletes and entertainers cross over. The question that always comes to my mind is would she be with him if he didn't have that contract? Or, what if he wasn't famous. The truth of the matter is that these white women would not be seen in public with them if they were not rich and famous. I mean, some of these athletes are rugged looking, to say the least, and if they think that these white women are with them, because of their character, without the status, black or white, they really need to think twice. The real point is, that in that world, crossing-over is acceptable and it's allowed! For example, take that famous running back, accused of killing his ex-wife and her lover.

Correct me if I'm wrong, but if memory serves me right, she was only sixteen when he met her as a waitress in some restaurant, and he was married. Now, I'm a parent and you tell me, if you were a parent, would you let your daughter date a married man and she was sixteen? More so, if you were a white parent and your daughter came home with a grown Black man and she was only sixteen, you would probably call the police. However, because he was who he was it wasn't a problem, evidently. Now look at the end results of that shit. You know what, ain't no *bitch* gonna be riding around in my shit, living in my mansion with some other *nigga* and think that shit is alright! I can't figure out for the life of me why you Black athletes run to these white women. Misdirected individuals, running, trying to be with white women, who would not give you a second look or time of the day, day of the week or month of the year if they saw you walking on the street. I will confess, however, that I have had one of my greatest sexual experiences with a white woman, and the first time I crossed over and had a relationship with a Hispanic woman, she took me to Puerto Rico. Ain't no black woman ever taken me anywhere that I didn't have to pay for her and me, except recently when my girl took me to England with her, even though I didn't want to go. On the other side of the coin are those fine sisters that are with these athletes. You and I know that they would never be with some of these athletes if it weren't about the money. Which brings me back to the Black man and his relationships with Black women. I remember the differences, very clearly. The attraction of Black women, when I started wearing suits as my basic attire, was like flies to shit. It's sad but true. They thought I had money, that's all! Same difference, when I went to those Texaco events and had to put on the Tux and those good ole *House Negro*es perpetrating as Christians, in church all week long, who thought I was somebody important. They all wanted to know who I was, and what I do for Texaco. *BASTARDS*! As soon as they see the less fortunate, homeless person or drug addict, they run as fast as they can to safety. They aren't trying to help no one. Not a damn soul. I hope come judgment day they get their just due. I pray he says 'I know you not'! Talk about poetic justice. I guess that's why so many people are scared of judgment day. They know their asses are going to hell. 'My people perish because of ignorance.' Hell, we can't even afford to live in Harlem anymore. Those *House Negro*es were so scared to be in Harlem after sundown that now white people run it. But for the *House Negro* that's not a problem. They sit around talking about the progress being made in Harlem. Yeah it's safe now, yeah it's cleaner now, yeah, there are a lot of developments going up, however, it ain't Black Harlem anymore. Fools! Only reason all these improvements especially increased security are taking place is because they are setting up shop for white people. I'll never forget the shock the first time I saw a white person get off the train late at night on125th street. That was unheard of, to say the least. It was like suicide. Now, you see more white people walking the streets of Harlem at night than ever before. Is there nothing sacred! I'm reminded of the story about

147

Nicodemus, when he asked Christ what he needed to do to enter into the Kingdom. When I think about the *House Negro* in that context, asking what they need to do to enter into the Kingdom and Christ tells them 'you need to go back to Africa', I can imagine them telling Christ to go to hell! Sounds a bit extreme I know, but that's how far they are from where they have come from. Some may wonder what the hell makes me so righteous, and judgmental. But I am warning those *House Negro*es/alleged Christians, to beware, because the detriment that they have caused our people will come back on them, and if there is anything that I can do to expose those useless, worthless sellouts, then my job and mission has been accomplished, and 'my living will not be in vain'. I will not stop until they are exposed for what they are, then maybe, just maybe, the world will look upon us with some sort of respect. But as long as they continue to be our voice, our representation, we are not going to be dealt with any differently than we continue to be dealt with, and that is not a future that is promising for any of our children. They will end up fighting the same fight I had to fight forty years after Martin Luther King and Malcolm X. It would be a sad testimony if in the 22nd century we are still, well, our children and their children, will still have to be fighting racism, and the ugliness and hazards that accompany it. So, it's not that I'm so righteous, I just am aware of the implications that stand before and beyond the generations afterwards if we don't purge those parasitical *House Negro*es from society. As I stated previously, I believe in the earlier chapter, that I spent a great deal of time after my formal learning, reading books like General MacArthur American Ceasar, General Patton Volumes l & ll, and General Eisenhowers Diaries and Supreme Commander, but the greatest learning, life changing experience came when I decided to study the Bible from an intellectual perspective. As I read, it challenged me like never before. It took me places I never would have or could have imagined. Actually I became a student of the Bible. It became the only book I would read. Every day it was more and more fascinating. What it actually did was change how I looked at the oppression my people were going through. I realized that it was those people who Jesus was concerned about. It was those people who Jesus cared for. It was those people who Jesus loved. You know, I thought I was exempt because I had a degree, but what I realized was that I probably wasn't one of those people Jesus loved or cared about. Not because I had a degree, but because of how arrogant and obnoxious I had become because I had a degree. All I knew was that if I was going to be anything of significance in this lifetime, I was going to have to take the test. The same test he gave to Nicodemus. I didn't have riches but I had a safety net. And he asked me, would I give up my safety net to walk with him? The test is really a simple yes or no test. I knew this was going to cost me big time! I probably was going to get thrown out the house by my mother, when I gave up my job, and decided to pursue this path, which seemed self-destructive. 'Oh, taste and see how wonderful he is'! Man he has brought me a mighty long way! He really changed me, and he changed the way I treat my fellow human being. That is why I can call those individuals walking around proclaiming to be Christians, hypocrites, because they treat their fellow man like garbage unless he is sporting a title or driving a Mercedes. I know for a fact that there were women who wouldn't date me because for a while I rode the bus to work. One in particularly, who was a devout Christian. Saved from the toes of her feet. I couldn't believe my ears the day her sister told me that she wouldn't talk to me because I rode the bus. I mean, I was crazy about this girl and she knew I was. I really had a thing for her. I believe, that shouldn't be the basis to determine whether you be with someone. So when I tell you how Black women treat the Black Man, believe it. When Black women get with a Black man, the vast majority of the time, it is to see what the man can do for them without them having to spend or contribute any of their resources. Let a Black woman see you in the day with sweat pants or dungarees and she is on her way to work, watch her reaction. Then let her see you in a suit anytime, night or day and see how she responds. That's why I say to those athletes and entertainers, the average looking ones, if you think she is there because of you, you better think again. That's just the way it is. Then they go around saying there ain't no good Black men out there. I say it's because their value system is all twisted. What they are saying is they can't find no sucker to put up with their trifling, misdirected mentality. So they end up crossing over. You should hear them. He treats me nice and he buys me things. That is their value system. They never stop to think that maybe if the white

150

man would employ a Black man and the disparities in income were not so extreme, that maybe the Black man could take her out and buy her things too, since that's how they translate caring. I wonder if they stopped to ask how that white individual deals with the Black men on the job who he probably supervises. Don't get me wrong, not all women are like that, but I am saying, virtuous women are few and far between. I don't remember my mother telling me you better shop around. I guess that was a job for my father but he wasn't nowhere to be found, actually he was dead by the time I was nineteen, killed in some fight over a women. Man, talk about irony.

As I began to explore this new life spiritually, I became totally amazed by the love, grace and mercy, and if I had not found it during that time period in my life, before Texaco, I would not have known how to handle that situation in Texaco. I knew that if God was for me, who could stand against me. I knew that my special book of Psalms would see me through. Even though times were rough, I really never felt the full wear and tear that that war exacted upon me. I mean these are the things that are written in the book. And time and time again, I have been in more trouble than a little bit and have watched the words come to life, to protect and direct me through the storm and the rain. Only now, as I really sit down and reconstruct this ordeal, I realize in totality the enormity of that ordeal. Many times I had told people that I was going to write a book about what really happened at Texaco, and they were gonna be surprised because it was not going to be a book solely about corporate bashing and exposing the racial inequality that everyone knows we are still facing till this very day in Corporate America, but it was going to be a book about those pitiful, disgraceful *House Negro*es and those who portrayed themselves as our representatives. That's the story I was gonna tell. Anyway, I was, still on my special assignment, wondering how long that was going to last, yet I was still the envy of many. By this time homeboy had to let me know that I still had to answer to him, so he came to me and told me that he needs a way to evaluate my performance in the department. He told me to come up with a project so he could evaluate and for me to make some type of presentation at the end of my assignment. I was like, damn, now I got to figure out some project to do, and boy oh boy did I come up with something so sweet that no one would have ever expected. I went to homeboy and said how about if I do a comparative analysis of Texaco's Foundation Grant Giving Program? You know, compare how much money Texaco gives to Whites, Blacks and Hispanics. He looked at me, and to my surprise he agreed. Actually he was very supportive. So, I started the process of ascertaining where and who had that information. That in itself became a very interesting project. It just so happened that this white boy who I used to play basketball with in our intramural league was the gatekeeper of the information. You would think that getting the information wouldn't be a problem. Right? Wrong! He did everything in his power to not compile that data for me. So, I asked and asked, and still nothing. When the Director, aka homeboy, would ask me how is my project going, at first I would say I am waiting for the data to be compiled by such and such. A little more time would pass, and he asked me again, and I would reply I should have it soon. Then I had enough and I went to homeboy and said, "you know he still hasn't gotten me this information and I have given him more than enough time to compile this data. I don't know what the problem is but maybe it would expedite matters if he got a directive from you. Know what I mean." And guess what? I soon had all the data. Interesting isn't it. Texaco probably should have been sued based on the disparity in its grant giving. The differential was enormous. I mean, just the money they gave to the Met exceeded all the money ten times over given to Blacks, Hispanics, Women, Indians, and Asians combined. The project was to give a Power Point presentation to the employees of Community Relations and a few executives of the department. Personally, I couldn't wait to begin my comparative analysis of this data. There it was in black and white, Texaco's Racist Giving. Actually, it was disgusting. So, as I began the categorization of the data, I came across this dilemma, with the title. Should it be titled Comparative Analysis of Whites vs. Minorities or Whites vs. Women and Minorities? The reason why I reference this is because when Texaco did their reporting of the numbers for the Courts, Women were included as minorities. Yet they are classified separately as Women. So which are they, Women or Minorities? They are Women. So then why are Blacks and Hispanics, even with the recent increase in the Hispanic population, called minorities? Why do we continue to let them classify us as such? I mean, to let someone classify you as minority is conceding inferiority. I smell those *House Negroes* somewhere in this conspiracy. I guess it coincides with the NAACP still being classified as Colored People. It's these types of psychological stigmas that still enslave us till this day. Just because there is a monetary value placed on being a minority by the government, we accept its justification. But if you realize, it ain't that much money and they have us fighting like animals for crumbs. So much so that Hispanics are now proud of being the leading minority. How the hell can someone be proud about that? This is just an example of the brainwashing that is going on and is keeping us from uniting. If Blacks and Hispanics united, we could control every election. But since the same old 'divide and conquer' tactics are still being employed till this very day, we remain in bondage. So here I have all this data. The white boy dropped it on me like, you want it, well here it is. You could tell that he was upset that he got a directive from homeboy who was Black, to do something. I think that was one of the biggest issues in Texaco, having someone Black telling you what to do. Since I never gave a Power Point presentation before I had to figure out how to do that. I know they were hoping I would fall on my face, but I was determined to put this data together and emerge successful, which of course I did. Even though I wasn't swimming upstream anymore, I felt like I was in the rapids. I had time, but I wasn't sure how much time I had to put this presentation together. What I did know was that I had resources and connections I could tap into to help me put it together. Ultimately I would have to be the one to put this data together. I got help from this white female in my old department, who was tech support, to assist me with how to do the Power Point presentation. Once I had accomplished that, I began putting pie charts, bar graphs, along with columns and rows of categories and statistics. I reserved the best room in the Conference Center that used to be reserved only for the Senior Level Executives, which remember, I used to be in charge of, to do my presentation. I told homeboy I was ordering breakfast, and he was like, "I 'm not so sure about that." I was like, "I am not having executives come to my presentation without giving them breakfast, at least coffee and danish." I used to do this for the meetings up there, so I just made a few phone calls and everything was taken care of. The view from the Conference Center was awesome. You could see the deer running through the grounds, and on a clear day you could see all the way down to New York City and it's skyline, which at that time had the twin towers. Everything in this room was automated. You could raise the blinds up and down for the windows, lower and raise the screen for the projector, dim the lights, you name it this room had it. State of the art. They thought I was going to do my presentation downstairs in one of the old conference rooms. They were in awe when they walked into the Conference Center. How'd you get this? Hell, I used to run this facility, that's how! The entire Community Relations Department was there, the special assistant to the CEO, the Head of the Foundation and a few others. Soon it was showtime.

Lights, Cameras, Action! You had to be there to really appreciate the set up. You had to know how Texaco was set up to understand the fabulous corporation that we were employed at. Since I used to run the facility, I already knew how to operate every piece of equipment, including the computer from the podium. Actually, you could run everything from the podium, lights and all. Just push a button. It was awesome. I had my laser pointer and was dressed in my new three-piece suit, new shirt, tie and shoes. I was 'in the house'. Many of the people from that department had never even been in the Conference Center. There I was, going through the numbers, explaining the differentiations and comparative implications. Not bragging, but I have always been good with numbers even from elementary school. It was the one area that I was superior to my white counterparts when I was thrust into integration in the mid sixties. The presentation went great even though I was a little nervous, especially since the numbers raised many concerns about Texaco's Foundation. One area that I expounded upon was the year after the lawsuit. The numbers were beginning to show a substantial decline in giving to Blacks, while on the other hand the contributions to white organizations were steadily increasing in dollar amounts and the number of white organizations contributed to. Interesting, to say the least. Yet all these Black organizations were still trying to get monies from Texaco, and the amount of monies available was constantly decreasing. Another area of interest was the contributions to Hispanics. The Hispanics were screaming bloody murder about the lawsuit and were just as angry as the whites that we were getting this money. They were saying we're minorities, like that was something to be proud of. Yet, the only reason they were screaming was because we got the money. During the lawsuit they never came to join us. Personally, I am tired of those who are only in this for the convenience. As far as I'm concerned, there is no difference between the *House Negro* and those who only want to be part of anything after the war is won. Anyway, Texaco had to quite the Hispanic Community, so the money that they were giving to us, they decided to take and give it to the Hispanics. Yet they never decreased any money they would give to the white organizations. So what does that create? It creates a division between the Blacks and Hispanics. We were fighting then and are still fighting now for the same money, so, inevitably we become enemies. Hopefully, this will open some of the minds and enable them to realize just how we are being manipulated for no real monetary value or gain. Something that really struck me and changed my approach to this whole comparative analysis, were the Asians and Indians. On one of my pie charts you couldn't even see where they were on the chart or the graph. I admit now, just as I did when I started my presentation to the group, that my sole purpose was to see the disparities in the giving to Blacks, but when I saw how bad it was for the Asians and Indians, I was like damn, they don't even exist. Probably the last area, which really struck a nerve, was on the giving to women in the health category. This was mainly because the Head of the Foundation was a woman. It's interesting how someone doesn't really become sensitive to the numbers until it affects them directly. And boy did it ever. Texaco's numbers showed a steady decline in monies to women over the last five years in health for women. She was outraged by this. However, the same indignation was not shared with the contemptible numbers in categories pertaining to Blacks with respect to the money that continually was decreasing and continued to increase for whites. Now why is that? See that's the problem. As long as we are not in any position to voice displeasure with the policy, they can always say, just like in the lawsuit, "oh, we didn't know." What a lousy excuse. After the presentation, she came to me asking for a copy of the presentation, mainly for the numbers where women were adversely affected. Nothing regarding the area where Blacks and Hispanics were concerned. I guess we were supposed to keep fighting over our minority status to validate or justify why one group deserves more than the other. Whoever needs the most pacification at the time would be the one who gets more from the designated pot allocated for minorities. Trust me, ain't no money gonna be taken from the pool that's dedicated to the whites. It was very humiliating to see that their numbers were never adversely affected throughout the five-year study I conducted. And even more to note, the money increased for them during Texaco's racial debacle. That just ain't right, it just ain't right. But you can see how the game is being played. We fight over crumbs while they continue to enjoy privileged status while simultaneously exploiting us. On the other hand, without knowing the data that exists and without mandating Texaco to release such data, hell, we don't even know we are being played like fools. They continue receiving the tax benefits from the government for their Giving, yet they ain't giving us nothing, at least nothing much to talk about, except a bunch of restrictions on how we must use the money. They are well aware of the areas where the money is needed in our communities, yet it's rare we ever receive the money for the most crucial needs to be met.   Again it's all a bunch of bull and we continue to fall for it.   There is something really wrong, when the attitude is oh well, who cares if we take the money designated for the Blacks and give it to the Hispanics.   You have to realize that these numbers are calculated, these numbers are reviewed and approved, they are approved by the CEO, CFO, and the Board of Directors. Don't believe that they are not aware that they are manipulating the money that is allocated for us.   Don't think they don't know that they have us fighting like animals for crumbs.   Also, don't think they don't know they increased the numbers for their own counterparts.   I received a serious ovation for my presentation. I was pleased that it went so well.   I must say it was impressive, from the room setup, to breakfast, from my Power Point presentation to my summation.   So what happens next after the congratulations and pats on the back? I'm back at my desk and I receive a phone call or maybe I saw him in passing, the Special assistant to the CEO who is now running the Public Relations Department, which Community Relations falls under.   I get the, when you get a minute I need to meet with you.   I would like to discuss your presentation. I'm like, here we go. You would think that since I met with him and all of that and now that he is heading up the Public Relations Department temporarily, I was straight. My colleague who was also in this program said, "you know if he wanted to, all he had to do was say, give Pete a position and it would be done." And you would think, after how well my presentation went that would be exactly what would be next. Right? Wrong!! Really wrong! So, I go into his office; he's no longer on Mahogany Row where all the executives sit. I guess they got tired of looking at him up there. I'm telling you, it was like that in Texaco. Actually, after they appointed the Head of the Diversity Task force to General Counsel, he was no longer the top Negro anymore. Believe me, I knew how things worked in there. I had to, after being there for twelve years now. I still acted like he was important, even though I knew he did not want the position running Public Relations. But that was as good as it was gonna get. They just used him to calm down those asinine *House Negro*es, fighting over the crumbs that weren't even there in the first place. The word was he was being put out to pasture. Anyway, I went in and as I sat down, he began criticizing my presentation, saying you know you can make numbers say anything you want. I replied I know that, and I knew that Texaco knew that, because that's exactly what they did when reporting to the Courts, via the Task Force that cost the plaintiffs $35,000,000.00. Just a side note, (I like putting down the actual numeric vs. written figure designated for the Task Force. It just has a different effect). I knew I was about to be sent back down stairs to my former department. Upon my return I was placed in Records Management, as a promotion. I don't know how going from Financial Planning to Records Management equated to a promotion, but that was my next assignment. Strange game, but I had to continue to play if I was going to survive. Before I left Community Relations I was able to secure funding for a computer technology center for the Boys & Girls Club in my community. Because of my role in Community Relations I was placed on their Board of Directors. Because of financial problems within Texaco, my Coach was soon relieved of his assignment working with me. Things were changing fast and once again I was becoming very concerned about my future at Texaco, but I had nowhere to turn to voice my concern. I definitely wouldn't go to the Diversity Task Force. One good thing that did happen was that the woman in Community Relations kept me in the loop, and would invite me to certain affairs that needed an African American. The Senior execs did not want to attend these events, like the Black Lawyers, and events that dealt with children in homeless shelters, like WestHelp. Personally, I enjoyed those activities. I also became part of the Toys for Tots drive at Texaco. I was doing pretty good even though I felt like I was being sabotaged. Going to Records Management with old storage boxes to be shipped out to a storage facility was not what I had in mind. All that was left to do was to bide my time and wait for the anticipated takeover of Texaco, and that's what I did. I was beginning to wonder, could a Black man ever get away from shipping boxes. Even when I was in a suit, they would ask me could I move this box. I would smile and say no problem. I was wondering if I was becoming a good *House Negro*. Don't bet your life on it, cause that ain't gonna ever happen.

Chapter 9

New Storm Brewing

So there I was, back in Corporate Services Records Management Department. Everyone in the department was wondering why I was back. From what I was told, Corporate Services was constantly crying, "when is Pete coming back. Remember he was only on loan." Hell, I didn't want to go back there because there wasn't "nothing" happening career-wise, that they had planned for me. They just wanted me back to deal with all those boxes that needed to be shipped out to storage in Tulsa, Oklahoma. As I previously stated, there was this woman, a white woman, who made sure I stayed in the loop with Community Relations. It damn sure wasn't the Black former special assistant to the CEO. Now I wonder why that was? You see, that's exactly what I am talking about. Here was a Black individual who could have intervened and made a difference in my career path at Texaco, yet for whatever reason, I was shipped back to a dead-end position in Corporate Services. Also, I will reiterate, it was two white men who arranged for me to become a permanent employee at Texaco. I will say this, however, it was a Black Woman who was in the employment office who got me in the door as a Temp. I'll tell you, if it wasn't for her, there probably would have been far less Blacks in that company. See, another Black female. She truly was a virtuous woman. When she left that position things sure did change drastically. It was over for us. We had no one to get us in the front door. Just like when I was selected to go through that evaluation, it wasn't until the white executive walked in and the former EEOC realized that he knew me and respected me, only then did he change his attitude. I guess all I am saying is that even though, systemically, the culture of the corporation was inherently discriminatory, the opportunities that I was afforded came because of the relationships that I had developed with whites. Now I wonder why that is? During my Temp years at Texaco, it was the Blacks who treated me like an outcast. It was the Blacks who wouldn't speak to me in the hallways when they were with white managers or white individuals from their departments. They would only attempt to speak to me when they realized that the whites they were with greeted me with such cordiality. It's those types of scenarios that make me have pure contempt for those individuals. You know, this wasn't just happening to me, it was, and is, happening to many Blacks, especially Black males who aren't considered acceptable because of their position in a company or their level of education. From the time I graduated from college, I basically worked as a Temp for various organizations, mostly fortune 500 companies, and for the most part the Blacks in those companies were just as disgusting as they were in Texaco. One common factor, other than the obvious, that the white man was in charge, was that everywhere I would go there was always that one so important Black person who would look at me as though I was poison. As I walked through different departments they would never say a simple hello, give any type of acknowledgement or want any affiliation of any kind to someone like me, simply because I was a

Temp. In a lot of the jobs I had in those companies I also wore suits, but I was looked upon as poison. It's these types of Negroes that are a major part of the problems we have as a race. Personally, I hate them. I guess I shouldn't, because if it weren't for them I probably would have never thought about writing a book in the first place. I always knew that if I decided to write a book about Texaco my main focus would be about how classless, and useless the Blacks involved in that lawsuit at Texaco were. No matter how I try to rationalize it, dissect it, Willie Lynch it, (again, for those of you who aren't aware of Willie Lynch, it basically was a concept created like Apartheid in South Africa, of how to control your slaves. You treat the lighter ones better than the darker ones.) Worked so well in South Africa that the light skinned ones wanted De Klerk to remain President of South Africa instead of Nelson Mandela. Just needed to reiterate! Can you even imagine something like that if you were white? Say for instance, you were being oppressed by some system and after years of imprisonment the leader of your people won his freedom and was now pushing for democracy for his people, and a certain group, because they had an incremental bit of favor, wanted the people responsible for maintaining this system of oppression to remain in power. What would you do? Knowing what I know, I guarantee, you would try to kill all those bastards! Actually, that would be the logical thing to do. This is why I say we need to kill them all! They are the ones who are destroying our race! And it is anyone like them, with that mentality that can and will destroy any race. Sure it was a white man who came up with the theory, but it was those ignorant fools who implemented the Willie Lynch theory better than the whites could have ever hoped for. They are and have been destroying our race for generations, especially today. I was surprised when I learned that the lighter Hispanics despised the darker ones. Why is it that we can't seem to understand the divisive tactics being instituted by the whites for their own personal gain at our expense? Do we desire to emulate them so much that to look like them and to be accepted by them is more important than our heritage? There needs to be a serious awareness campaign to help us understand that we all need to work together if we're going to be successful. When I say we, I mean all those who have been exploited for the white race's personal gain. And that's most of the world. I remember one day visiting one of my childhood friend's college in Long Island. I mention this because there was this Black History class that I went to while I was there visiting. There definitely was no such course where I went to college. Basically, I was fascinated that it even existed. What was interesting, however, was when the professor, who was a Black female, (something else that was non existent where I went to college) spoke about Coups and revolutions in African nations, and how the new government would basically end up just as, or in most cases, more corrupt than the governments they replaced. Listening with disappointment, I raised my hand to ask a question. She finally acknowledged me and allowed me to ask my question. My question to her was, "does this mean given all the facts about how most of these coups turn out, do you think it is possible for us to have a successful revolution?" She replied, "given the outcomes to date, probably not." As I think back to that question and as I relate it to all I have experienced in the last twenty-five years, a quarter of a century no less, looking at Africa, looking at us in America, looking at the social unrest and injustice, I actually don't know if we can go around and survive off of a 'keep hope alive slogan'. I mean, we still make up the vast majority of the prison population in this country. We still remain the highest unemployed group. Our inner city schools are failing to educate, yet I submit to you as an intellect, and one who has mentored and taught, that education begins at home, with or without both parents. I also submit that racism is taught at home. Discrimination is learned through racist teaching. I personally am at the point where I believe that the only hope for us is that God saves us from this path of destruction that we continue to head down with ever increasing vigor. Without proper education we as a people will not survive, you best believe that! Education is the only tool that can free us. So I caution the youth not to look at education as the tool for a good job, cause that was the myth that was sold to me when I went to college. Understand that education is knowledge. Education is like having the power to destroy all barriers in your way, be it human or otherwise. Once you are armed with education, you won't fall for the theories instituted like Willie Lynch. However, if you get an education just for the benefits of a good job, you will be missing the true purpose of why our ancestors fought so hard to make sure that we were educated. It was to make sure that our white adversaries would not be able to take advantage of us. But you see what can happen when you empower one ignorant *House Negro* over his own people. He will make sure that the Willie Lynch theory is implemented to the fullest extent of the law, so to speak. And that is where we are this very day in the twenty first century. The white man 'damn near don't have to do a damn thing'. He has the *House Negro*. The *House Negro* is and always will be a detriment to our race. He will sell us, and his mother out faster than a slave running from the hound dogs in the woods. Of course you know that it was the *House Negro* who told *massa* in the first place, that you ran away. You know if there comes a day for retributions to be made for slavery, my wish would be to put those *House Negro*es on trial for being traitors, which is a crime punishable by execution. That's the only thing I can think of to do with them at this time. Even my spirituality won't allow me to forgive those traitorous bastards. Do you realize the price it has cost our race? Do you realize the death and despair and the countless beatings that were inflicted upon us because that *House Negro* went back to *massa* and sold us out? I'll never forget the story about how the initial lawsuit sought against Texaco got sabotaged and the only Black lawyer in the company was terminated. Somebody went and told and he was fired on the pretext of conflict of interest. Nobody white knew, or was supposed to know. So, who the hell does that leave? Some dumb ass black *nigga, who* went and talked to some white person thinking that they supported our cause, this is just hypothetical, however, logic does prevail. You know how the whites are portrayed in the movies, that 'Great White Hope' syndrome, gonna save the poor dumb Black folks. I don't know about you, but I am sick of it, and it is my very intention to expose those who are responsible for this. Trust me, it ain't the poor Blacks who are struggling every day trying to survive who are responsible for this. They know who the culprit is behind their oppression. That is why I find the streets refreshing. To me, having the respect from the streets is important because it reassures me that I am still in touch with the struggle of my people. I don't ever want to lose that no matter how important I become. It is paramount to me that I can communicate with them and they can communicate with me. You see it is a real simple concept. It's called RESPECT! We better learn that just because an individual doesn't have the material amenities of this world, that he is no lesser a human being. The irony of all of this is that most of these Negroes that have these material possessions go to church every Sunday praising and thanking God. Everywhere you see them and you ask them how are they doing, they respond 'God is good and I'm blessed'. But yet they still look down upon the less fortunate. They despise the poor. Everything that Jesus represented and taught, they are totally contrary to. I find it simply amazing. On the other hand, the street mentality, which is just as misdirected, glorifying getting shot and/or going to jail as rites of passage to being a man is just as sick. As long as we continue down this road of destructive interaction, we will continue to lead in all the categories

169

like uneducated, underemployed unemployed, incarceration and death at earlier ages than any other race. Yeah, I know you will say, well it's not me and that doesn't pertain to me, so I really don't care. It's that type of mentality that is also destroying us. Ironically, however, when the police shoots and kill one of you House Negroes who think that you are not in the classification of the Black race and it's ills and misfortunes, then you're crying racism and looking for justice. And when you don't get any justice, you want Reverend Al, that same Black individual you used to call a big mouth and ignorant, to come and speak out against these white people who you love so much and want to emulate so desperately. Yet if it happens to some poor underprivileged, uneducated, unemployed Black youth, all of a sudden you could care less. You don't even recognize that the reason it happened to him is because in their eyes we are all the same. So, as long as you believe that you have some type of immunity from the ills that affect the poor Black, and not you, because you are middle class or higher, you will be in for a very rude awakening. I'll tell you one thing, if you get stopped in the South on a lonely highway you better start praying, because it might be your last opportunity to pray, mister high and mighty, uppity *House Negro*. Instead of embracing and respecting someone who has the courage to stand up and confront the brutality encountered by our people at the hand of the police, you chose to degrade that individual who was victimized and detach yourself from any association and/or affiliation. For you to associate with someone like that would be considered unacceptable by your white associates, and fellow comrades of the white value system. It is a shame that you feel so removed from the plight and the everyday struggle of your people. Actually, it is disgraceful. You are a disgrace to our race and to our heritage. When Martin was alive he would always ask the question, 'how long'? He would ask it in that context because we were constantly, and still are being grossly mistreated by whites in this country. Now that you have finally gotten a piece of the pie, and life is allegedly good, you don't want to hear no speeches about 'how long'. My question to you is, 'how long'? 'How long' will you continue to be an ignorant *House Negro*? 'How long' will you continue to deny your heritage? 'How long' will you continue to treat your fellow brethren as less than human? Hell, if you're doing it, what makes you think that whites will ever stop doing it? You do it at work in front of the white man, you do it at church, and you do it in the streets. Everyone knows and everyone sees. God help you if you ever get laid off from the plantation. I sure would like to know what you're gonna do. Personally, I feel sorry for you. But then again it would serve you right. Sort of a poetic type of justice.

I remember when an old friend of mine got his first job after college with that company that swore you had a job for life. I remember he started as a Temp working in the mail- room. Yeah, another Black male, college graduate, and the only position in Corporate America available was a temp assignment in the mailroom. He was going through all kinds of changes. All I used to tell him was stay professional. When he finally became a permanent employee, we no longer communicated. There were no more of those long in- depth conversations about the outright sabotage of Black males, especially Black educated males. Yeah, my homeboy from the Projects turned. He was accepted now. He finally got his piece of the pie. The irony is that he probably had no idea that he changed. The difference between us was that people from the old school would always ask me "what's up with your boy?" I would say, "I guess you could say he moved to a better plantation, ain't got time for people like us no more." They would say, "but you graduated from college and you work for a good company, yet you still are a part of us." My answer would be, "maybe he's ashamed of where he came from." So I know first hand how these things happen. I mean, we used to talk about how alienated we felt by our families since we graduated from college. It was almost like they were mad at us for something we accomplished. It was really strange. People would always comment about us graduating from college. Then again, there were many that went and soon returned home to never go back, yet they were like heroes in the hood. The streets are strange. Growing up in the Projects was, and is still, very interesting from a sociological perspective. I remember in high school how the people that had houses, who lived on the other side of town, would not allow their daughters to talk to us. Sought of a West Side Story. They would also be damned if we were coming to their house, like we were some type of poison. The Northside Boys Club vs. the Southside Boys

Club, the Southside being where the poor Blacks were from. It was still Black against Black. Social and economic division even then, yet there was only one high school, so we had no choice but to encounter each other in the hallways at school. What I realized was that it wasn't us, it was the parents who had the problem. Does owning a house vs. not, make someone better than someone else? I suggest that that is a poor man's mentality, Black or White. That's the mentality of someone who never had anything in life in the first place. And when you think about it, most of the people who came here in the first place didn't have a damn thing anyway. They all came to Ellis Island with nothing but the clothes on their back. Couldn't speak English, couldn't read and/or write. Somehow we internalized the mentality of those who had nothing in the first place. If we knew where we came from, and how great a people we were before we fell from the grace of God and into slavery, we would definitely, hopefully, treat each other different. However, since the system was designed to keep us divided through theories like Willie Lynch, we sink like we're walking in quicksand. The more we struggle the faster we sink. You would think that our fellow man would tell us to watch out, there is quicksand over there. Instead, he turns his back and watches us walk right into the quicksand. You would think that our fellow brethren, when he sees his fellow man sinking in the quicksand, he would throw him a rope. Instead he turns his back and walks the other way. The same applies to how we were enslaved in the first place. Tribe against tribe, we got played just like a fiddle by the white man. I hate you because, not even knowing why. I can't help you because you're darker than me. I can't help you because you live on the Southside. I remember one day after church, my old friend and I had a conversation. He was no longer employed at the company where you had a job for life. He shared something very provocative with me about a church across the street from the Projects. I shared with him that I like to go there for Bible Study. He said to me, "Pete, remember when we were kids, did any of us ever go inside that church?" I was dumbfounded. But he was absolutely right. There were five hundred families in the Projects, yet we went to every church except that one. He then educated me to the fact that 'we didn't belong.' It wasn't for us. Now, everybody from the Projects and their Grandma goes there. Incredible! I thought. I wondered if it was because it was a Methodist church and we were mostly Baptist. It was still shocking, the divisiveness that lives in religion. Maybe it's religion that is the greatest divider of man, not Willie Lynch. Wow! What a revelation! I make this point to again raise the issue of how we interface and interact with each other as a class and as a race. I can't help but feel that, united, we would have never left Africa. United, we would not be walking around here with these damn slave names. When I stop to think and review history and process the information and consider what happened to us as a people, I stop and ask myself who am I? Really, think about it. Who the hell am I? What is my real name? Who are my ancestors? Do you realize that we are the only group of people in the world who do not know who we are, and where the hell we come from? If I'm wrong please tell me. Yeah, the white man took us. That is what we think or believe. I know that's what I used to believe until a read a book that informed me that the biggest perpetrators of the slave trade were the Portuguese. I didn't even realize that until a few years ago. I always believed that it happened the way it happened on 'Roots', the television show. Yeah, the white man took us, but for the most part it was a trade, a betrayal by our leaders against their own people, a betrayal by our leaders against each other. For the most part we were sold into slavery, not stolen from our land. Takes me right back to where we are today. Those sell outs, those Traitorous *House Negroes*. They have inflicted irreparable damage on our race then and now. I am not sure what case can really be made for reparations if, in fact, we were traded. Makes it a little more difficult. Anyway, even if we did win reparations, I guarantee you, the only ones that would profit would be the lawyers. There would be so many stipulations we wouldn't even know where to begin to collect the money we would be entitled to. Trust me on that one, especially after the Texaco settlement. We won, but we really lost in the long run.

Some say we should go back to Africa, but there is such unrest going on there, including genocide, right now in the 21st century. Will they ever wake up and realize that as long as they continue down this path of destruction and despair, we will never reemerge to our once great status of respect in the world. I remember one evening going out to dinner in New York City with a lady friend of mine and this African waiter came over to the table trying to impress my date. (This is what I have been waiting to tell you about). I watched for a while, then, I decided to check the brother because now he was being a bit disrespectful. He was about to learn a valuable lesson from me and about me. I will check you whether you're Black or White. I may tolerate the ignorance from a Black person a little bit longer than a White person, but when I have had enough you will definitely know about it. So, as he continued about how wonderful it is in his country, I simply interrupted and asked, "if it's so god damn wonderful there, then why the hell are you here?" You should have seen the look on his face. Yeah, that's right, then why the hell are you here? Then the truth came out about all the political infighting and how if he stayed his life might be in jeopardy. I looked at him and smiled and with anger replied, "you are still doing the same damn things that put us into slavery in the first place." Of course my dialogue was a bit different, but my point was that this was the same ignorance that basically was the cause of us being brought over here as slaves in the first place. Ain't a damn thing changed. This is why Africa the continent is still being raped of its resources and exploited every day. I remember working as a Temp in a bank in lower Manhattan near the former World Trade Center. I remember preparing the proxy statements that needed to go out to the customers. All these quarterly reports for the Diamond Mines and the Gold Mines in South Africa. That's why I say to the Rappers, why you making the white man rich, sporting all that gold and all those diamonds that come from the blood of your brothers in Africa. At least, if you're going to sport it, be smart about it. Invest in Gold. Buy a Diamond mine. Hell, with all the money all of you are making, you could buy your own country. Do you feel me? Why do you think they let you get on T.V. and perpetrate like that? Now all the younger kids want to buy gold chains and diamond rings. At least if they are going to try and use you, use them back. Just like FUBU. Have a diamond mine named after a group of all of you. That way, they will be buying all the gold and diamonds from you. That way you can pay the brothers that are being exploited in the diamond and gold mines a decent wage, so they can take care of their families. Get the picture. You have the power to build, so don't let them fool you, and more so, don't let them continue to play you like a sucker. While I was working for this bank down by the World trade, this country, America, was not even supposed to be doing business with any company that supported apartheid. Let me tell you, we were shipping out so much material we had to work overtime for months, upstairs in the mailing and downstairs in shipping, nothing but exploitation all around. We were slaving, and the ones in the mines were definitely slaving. Modernized slavery here vs. good ole fashion slavery over there in Africa. I also recall when I worked Temp for a Defense Contractor when good ole boy Ronnie was president of the U.S. and Gorbachev, was president of Russia. They were meeting to discuss the Nuclear Non-Proliferation Treaty. Let me tell you, it is interesting what takes place in those positions at the bottom, because that's where all the

177

work has to be done. So while they were discussing arms reduction, the new orders for building military weapons were coming in like a hurricane had landed. Orders and more orders. That's when I was working in the Reproduction Room. That's where all the blueprints were developed and processed for the engineers. Didn't pay worth a damn, but I saw it all. I was saying what a sham this whole arms reduction treaty is. I guess Russia was over there doing the same as we were. The exploits continue at every level you can imagine and at levels you can't even begin to conceive. But the level of exploitation that continues till this very day in Africa by Africans is disgusting. We know the whites are covertly or overtly operating over there, still we do nothing about it, and even worse we don't even say anything about it. I guess to say something about it 'may end you up dead'. I think that is why we really don't have any real leaders in comparison to Malcolm and Martin. Make no mistake about it, if you step out too far they will put a bullet in your skull. What's probably even worse is that our own people will actually create the opportunity for it to happen. Right now all I can do is shake my head, because the more I expound on the issues that have brought us to these crossroads, I fear that the solution is in some type of quadratic formula that's gonna take a Ph.D or better to try to bring us out of this path of self destruction. The only other solution that I see as a formidable solution is "The End". "The final Chapter", Revelations! As an Economics major I don't see economics changing it. I don't see us socially uniting to change it. The church is damn near in ruins, since they have become the new Corporate America. The church is bigger than big business. But when all is said and done, the only thing that logistically has any dominion, has any credence regarding a true change, is the separating of the wheat from the tare, the purging of, the purification of, in essence, the extinction or extermination of the *House Negro*. THANK YOU LORD! Oh Happy Day! Just imagine if we could turn back the hands of time. No *House Negro*es. Can you begin to imagine what kind of world this could have been? Since our enslavement began as trade, first and foremost we would have never been for sale. Mother Africa would have never been breached and raped. We would still be kings and queens. I guess the white people don't want to imagine this because who would they have to cut the sugar cane and pick the cotton and tobacco for them so they could live their life of privilege? Who would work the diamond mines and gold mines for their wealth, etc. Some believe it was God's will for us to be their slaves, so they could be afforded this life. Look at the Pharaohs of Egypt. They killed, tortured, exploited for their privileged life, yet Rome is considered one of the greatest empires to ever bless the face of the Earth. It's sick, just sick. As I go through my visions of utopia on earth, which ain't gonna never happen, I guess it is necessary to attempt to put this *House Negro* into some type of perspective other than how he's been portrayed thus far. And as I thought about it, and as I journeyed back to the days of Egypt, I thought about Moses and how he went to Pharaoh and demanded the freedom of his people. But do you remember that character Dathan, the one who found out Moses' secret about being a Hebrew? Remember how he sold his soul to the Egyptians to prosper, and how in the movie, 'The Ten Commandments', he was trying to convince the people that they were better off under the care of Pharaoh. Remember the golden calf? The *House Negro* wreaks of the stench of that character. They are synonymous. Dathan would say, we were better off as slaves with Pharaoh. The *House Negro* would say, we got a good *massa,* I'm gonna tell if you try to run away. All in all, by any means necessary for himself to benefit, the *House Negro,* like Dathan would do just about anything to gain favor with their masters. It's a sad testament of a man. Dathan convinced them to build a calf in the wilderness, he almost convinced them that they were better off in Egypt under the whip of the taskmasters. Thank God for Moses. Imagine what it would have been like if there wasn't a Moses. See, we had our Moses in Malcolm and in King, even though we didn't appreciate Malcolm when he was alive. There was a reason why they killed Malcolm first. They knew that all hell would have broken loose if they had killed King first, cause Malcolm would have had a field day with the press about the violence that the white people continue to inflict on Blacks. They knew Martin would vow for non-violence after they killed Malcolm. Here again, those Judas Iscariots were at work. Oh, the irreparable damage the *House Negro* has inflicted upon the Black Race. There is not an ounce of difference between Dathan in Egypt and the *House Negro* in America, or for that fact the traitors in Africa. They are cancerous, and without strong leadership they can destroy every positive accomplishment and drag it under the ground. Do you think for a moment that if Malcolm and/or Martin were still alive today that we would be in this predicament? Hell no! We wouldn't have these so-called bogus individuals calling themselves leaders. Those *House Negro*es would have been purged from our race. And Black pride would still be the standard. There probably would have never been a Texaco Class Action Lawsuit because all these injustices and indifferences would have been addressed. Trust me, this was a well thought out process. They knew once they got rid of Malcolm and King, it would set us back generations. Don't forget we still need approval to vote. It's a Voting Rights Act that has to be approved by thirty-eight states. What a disgrace. Malcolm and Martin can never rest in peace looking at the disarray we face today. We really need to consider purging our race. Do you know why they separate the wheat from the tare? They separate the wheat from the tare because the tare would grow and ultimately choke and kill the wheat. Do you know what they do with the tare once it's separated from the wheat? They burn it. So look at the *House Negro* as the tare, except he hasn't been burned, so all he does is continue to grow, choke and destroy his people like the tare when it is not separated from the wheat. But I am here to tell you that there is going to come a day, a day of reckoning, and guess what *House Negro*, may you burn in hell for all the travesties and tragedies that you have aided and abetted the enemy with, in our captivity and enslavement. May your ancestors from the Motherland who partook in our captivity and enslavement burn endlessly in the unquenchable fires of hell written in the book of Revelations. Burn like the tare that you are. The only reason you have survived this long is because you continue to choke the life and hopes out of our people. I pray for judgment to come upon you swiftly, for the crimes that you have committed against your own people, the damage that you have caused to our race. The destruction that was inflicted upon us could have only been achieved through your hands. I guess you modernized *House Negro*es are glad that it is damn near impossible to trace all the way back to the beginning of this crime because then we would be able to gather the evidence of your ancestors' responsibility for this horrific and tragic act. Maybe we should crucify you. We must, by any and all means necessary, get rid of this cancer in our race. Look at us, and where we are in the 21st century. Take a good look at the people in New Orleans. Yeah, Hurricane Katrina was devastating, but look at how they were living before the hurricane. Go around the corner from the White *House* or the Capitol in Washington D.C., there is a ghetto like you would not believe. Oh, I have to take that back. Just recently visited and it has improved, at least on the outside. I never could figure out how diplomats could come to this country and not see the poverty right here in good ole America, right in the Nations' Capitol, no less. Nevertheless, realize that the people who are supposed to represent us, and fight for opportunities for us, are unaccounted for. Where are they? How come we are living like animals, impoverished and suffering, after all that we have contributed to this great society? I've heard it said that others now do the work that we don't want to do. Well, for four hundred years we did the work that many groups were not even strong enough to do! So, for whoever said that, they can go to hell too! Let's set the record straight here once and for all! When we were brought here against our will, key word here is 'against', they did everything to ensure we stayed illiterate, uneducated, and subservient. Everyone else who came here, came of their own free will to escape a horrific political climate or economic situation. We weren't allowed to go to school, we weren't given any employment opportunities, and every means necessary to degrade and exploit us was utilized. Yet we still learned, became doctors, lawyers, engineers, and anything else you can think of, in spite of everything. We didn't have signs translated into our language because we couldn't read or speak English! So before you start going around talking that nonsense, make sure you know what the hell you are talking about. Before you talk about a man, make sure you walk a mile in his shoes first. How many of you could have survived what we went through? Show some damn respect! We built Pyramids that they can't even figure out to this very day how to build! Let me see anyone of you who feel so superior, build a pyramid, in the desert heat of Africa. It's tragic what happened to a people once so great, but don't try to add salt to the wound, you may not like what you get in response. Don't try to elevate yourself on the pain and suffering of one group of people to benefit yourself. I know that the temptation to do so is there, especially when you look and see how we treat each other. Don't pile on because that's what everybody else is doing. Don't become the tare like the *House Negro*, for surely judgment awaits all. Don't try to choke us, and then try to act like you are superior because you have gained favor with our exploiter. Surely we will become enemies. But realize that their end product is to divide and conquer us. For united we cannot be controlled. Stop fighting over the crumbs from the table. That is exactly what Texaco did between the Blacks and Hispanics after the lawsuit. Remember the comparative analysis presentation? The numbers showed without a doubt that the money once designed for Blacks was now being directed to the Hispanics, yet the money for the whites was continuing to increase? You must realize the bigger picture. Why wouldn't they take some money from the whites to give to the Hispanics, considering that the whites were already getting millions more than any other group? Why? You need to understand this if nothing else! Instead they chose to take the money from the funds allocated for the Blacks who weren't getting much of anything in the first place. Yet even when the lawsuit first was settled and the money for Texaco to focus specifically on doing business with Blacks was increased, they never made any downward adjustments from any white organization. Yet, when they were forced to give Hispanics some of the pie because of the cries from the Hispanic population, they took it from the Blacks. Now as then, they have us fighting over these crumbs. They never fight over crumbs. You better open your eyes! Same thing applied when the CEO allegedly leveled the playing field for me.

Everyone was acting so pleased and thrilled about these opportunities that were to materialize. One would think that I should have been grateful and happy that this was happening to me, yet I was smart enough to know that I needed to remain cautious and careful, because one slip and it would have been over. Actually, I became even more gangster, as I played the game, because I knew that there was a new storm brewing on the horizon, and Texaco was about to catch my wrath once again. One thing my Coach taught me was to keep the fire alive inside. And so I did, and here we were about to go again. It was time for my evaluation from the Corporate Services Department, now in Records Management, and we now have a new supervisor. Before I tell you about that, let me tell you about the original supervisor. She was a pleasant woman to work with. I guess after everything I had been through with my Black female supervisor, this white woman was a breath of fresh air. Actually, it was a pleasure to work with someone who was educated and respected my style, effectiveness and efficiency. Shortly after, she informed me she was leaving to go into a position in the Financial Planning Group, my old group. A promotion no doubt, especially since they were promoting white women all throughout Texaco. That is actually how they were able to comply with the requirements of the Court from the lawsuit. Isn't it interesting how a lawsuit for us ended up benefiting everyone else except us. All of a sudden everything is diversity. But when you look at the Board of Directors and you look at the Senior Management, ain't no damn diversity going on up there. And we like fools buy that garbage. Anyway, she went on to say that she doesn't know who's going to replace her, etc. She then tells me what a great job I have done and all that garbage even though I do believe she was sincere. So I went on to write in my evaluation about how this department continuously praises me for the great work I do but when it comes to putting me in charge of an area that I am doing so well in, and definitely more than qualified to run, there always seems to be a problem. Hell, I have the experience, and the education. I've been working for this company for almost, ten years or more. What the hell does this *nigga* boy need to do to get a position commensurate with his education, experience and time served within this damn Organization? Of course she called me in, after receiving my response and told me she agrees with me, however, I shouldn't say things like that, at least not on record. I said "yeah I know, but you know." It was obvious that nothing had changed. My Coach used to say to me that "the more things changed the more they stayed the same." I felt like that Confucius saying, if a tree falls in the forest does anybody hear? Well I will tell you this, there wasn't anybody there to hear. There was no one I could turn to, to plead my case with. The Head of the Task Force was now Texaco's General Counsel, I damn sure couldn't go and talk to him about it. Wasn't no cameras, so that group that still call themselves Colored People was nowhere to be found. Definitely wasn't no Rainbow in sight. The attorneys were mad because they didn't get the settlement they desired, so they were through. Ain't no need in writing to the CEO, but the thought did cross my mind. I was stuck between a rock and a hard place, to put it mildly. So the new supervisor was finally brought in. I know him, but not that well. The word was that his father used to be this big time executive in one of the operating departments of Texaco, but nobody wanted his son, so he ended up in Corporate Services. That may or may not have been true, but whatever it was he had been with the company for twenty plus years, so there wasn't anything I could say about him having the opportunity to run Records. Hell, he deserved the opportunity. So I put my personal feelings aside and worked to make Records as good as it could be, much to everybody's surprise. I became the consummate team player. And things were running pretty smooth for now. Just one note about operating departments vs. service departments, when one becomes assistant to the CEO, at least at Texaco, the objective is to run major operations. Not the garbage that they had the Black Assistant to the CEO doing. When you become assistant to the CEO at Texaco you are in the major meetings with the Senior Level Executives. I know because I used to run the Conference Center where they met. Trust me, he was never there. So all the hoop-la going on about how Texaco was doing this and that by these misguided Black individuals, was nothing more than a diversion from what was really going on. A crumb here and a crumb there was all that was happening and they were satisfied. No questions, nothing. What a sorry group of people. At least the so-called uneducated street Negro would have known he was being shammed. As Malcolm used to say, 'you've been hoodwinked'. Those *House Negro*es are just born suckers. They fall for everything and anything, just like they did back in Africa. One of the books that I was reading called the Slave Trade, by Hugh Thomas, told of one of the leaders selling his people for a shaving bowl. What an idiot! Stupid! And you know what else, as I walk in the Caribbean Islands and I see who owns all the Hotels and land and see the poverty that the people are surrounded by outside of the resort areas, it angers me. We need to find a way to take back what is ours. But until the ones who are in government stop selling us out by making the same kinds of deals, like a shaving bowl for a human being, we will continue to live in this world of hopelessness and despair. I will say, I do admire what Chavez is doing in Venezuela. He is controlling the resources of his country. Imagine if in Africa we would take back control of our resources, the diamonds, the gold, the iron-ore, the precious minerals. As for now, only a few are benefiting from these deals made with the same culprits or descendants of the same culprits who enslaved us in the first place. I have come to the conclusion that for the most part we as a people are horrible in the field of business. You know, everybody thinks that they can run their own business and be entrepreneurs, but there is serious work that goes into running a business and I don't know any other way to explain our situation because of the horrible deals we continue to make in the name of our people. Our singers and entertainers end up broke or die broke because of contracts they negotiated, or someone else negotiated for them. Look at the Texaco settlement. It was a damn fiasco. When was the last time anything was negotiated that benefited Blacks. I personally am at a loss. I can't think of anything. Look at Hurricane Katrina. Look at our schools in the inner cities. Look at the abuse we suffer in the judicial system. I mean the list goes on and on. Our children are dying. We lead the polls in AIDS. We lead in everything negative you can imagine. Where is our leadership crying out, representing us? Yet, if you ask the *House Negro,* he will tell you everything is good and how he is blessed. How can someone feel blessed when our children are dying and being abused? Easily! You just turn the other cheek! Our Churches should be raising holy hell about what is happening to us in this society and throughout the world. That's why when the CEO supposedly leveled the playing field for me I wasn't singing hallelujah, because I knew that the majority of Blacks, what few were left in the company, were still catching hell. So as far as I was concerned there was still a war going on. There I was still fighting, but fighting smarter and more strategically. I was picking my battles with tact and precision. People were surprised that after all the hell I raised that I was still with the company, because everyone else was for the most part neutralized or terminated. I was really the last plaintiff standing. War was on the horizon, and if you know anything about me since reading this story, I like war. Soon it was time for another yearly evaluation. I was determined that I was not going to settle for anything less than a 'strong', which was the second highest rating next to being excellent. Actually, only about five percent of the company even qualifies for that category. So there I was with my new supervisor discussing what and why I feel I should be a 'strong'. So I let him know why. He said he agreed, but upstairs would have to approve it. I knew all hell was about to break loose. Many of the allies that I had won over upstairs had retired from the department and now we had a fresh bunch of 'red necks' that were in charge of the department. It didn't take long before I got the call to come upstairs to have a discussion about my review. I knew I was doing extraordinary work since my resurrection from the lawsuit with my Coach. I was mentoring seventh and eighth graders for a local middle school, I was part of this program where we would talk to high school students about making the transition from high school to college and the work force, and the importance of education. I was on the Board of Directors for the Boys and Girls Club in my community and got the necessary funding through Texaco to help build a technology center there. I was working with Westhelp, a homeless shelter, and I did Toys for Tots. I had become a really good 'Corporate Citizen'. I trained various departments on the new computerized system for Records Management, the second time I had to train Departments on a new system. I had perfect attendance for two maybe three years in a row. The list was impressive, but when it went upstairs the new 'red neck' told me that he's not giving anybody a strong. I tried to explain to him that this was part of a process, a special assignment that was approved by the CEO, but he didn't care. He told me I could appeal it, but you and I know that the process was bogus. I did appeal it and the people who were to make that decision were biased, I knew it and so did that fat sloppy ass 'redneck'. What they didn't know was that after working ten years with a company, one does begin to know the system. So I went back door and used my whole card on that redneck's ass. There was a new storm brewing, and I was about to claim another racist's neck for my trophy case. After the lawsuit, the CEO created this position called the Omnsbud person, who was responsible for hearing the concerns of any employee of the company. She was located out of the Houston office, however, she used to work at the Corporate Headquarters in White Plains. Actually, she was a Black woman who was always decent and treated everyone with respect. See, another Black woman! Not every Black woman is useless, however, virtuous, well that's another story. Black women used to be queens, but that was a different generation of women! The Omnsbud person was always pleasant and one of the few Blacks who always would speak to a brother whenever or whoever she was with. She was also very attractive, and as we say in the "Hood", she was fine! So I gave her a call down in Houston and explained everything that was going on. She was very interested and I said to her, I don't understand what the problem could be unless this was some type of retribution for being in the lawsuit. I sent her documentation and she began looking into it. She was actually very impressed with my accomplishments and had asked if being involved with all these different activities affect my primary responsibilities. I told her what my responsibilities were and how I was training the entire Corporate

Headquarters in the new computerized system for Records Management. She replied to me, "this is exactly the type of performance that the company is trying to develop in its employees." I said, well, how come you see this yet this asshole, (I didn't really say asshole) but how come he couldn't see it. Where exactly was the disconnect? She told me she would investigate and get back to me. (Now imagine if I would have let that other evaluation be placed in my records from that other Black female who was my supervisor)? Some time had passed and I decided to give her a call to check on the status of the investigation. She traveled a lot so it took longer than I had expected, however, when she did get back to me, she said, "to expect a call any day from upstairs." She said, "that's all I can say." I was not sure how this was going to play out, but sure enough, I got the call from upstairs that the 'redneck' wanted to meet with me. So he came downstairs, and I'll tell you this, I will never forget the look of hate on that redneck's face when he came downstairs. I tried to warn him but he wouldn't listen. It was like in the NFL when they throw the red flag onto the field to protest a bad call by the referee. It was like, after further review we are going to change your rating to a 'strong'. He couldn't even say the words, but he had no choice. They had to change my raise, my benefits, everything. The only thing was that Texaco was soon to be acquired by Chevron. People were saying why bother, and I would say it's the principle. If it didn't matter that much then why were they hell bent on making sure I didn't get it? As far as I was concerned, it was just another victory against these racist bastards, and that is the difference between myself and the *House Negro*. The *House Negro*, first of all, would never have challenged what the white man gave him. He would just say 'thank you *massa'*. I was more like kiss my ass you racist bastard. Hell, I was actually making Texaco look good. But make no mistake about it, when I talked to the youth about what it was like being in that lawsuit against Texaco, I never hesitated to tell them the real deal. I would explain to them that if it wasn't for my education I wouldn't have had a leg to stand on. Like most of the Black employees there, many hadn't had any formal education of higher learning. If they did they probably would have been able to take a stand. So I re-emphasize to the youth how important it is to get an education because you need it if you're going to be able to fight the injustices you face in this game in Corporate America. I used my education to tell many employers to kiss where the sun don't shine. Might not have been the wisest thing to do, but I sure got gratification from it. I knew that I could always get another job because of my education. May not have been the job I wanted but a job, is a job, is a job. The problems develop when you start looking for career opportunities. And these immigrants who are not legal yet, when they have to start paying taxes, and start needing more money to survive in this country and want their fair share, and want higher wages, they are going to be in for a rude awakening. Not because of the color of their skin, because their skin is not black, but when they start infringing on the opportunities for the whites, especially the white males, things are going to become mighty different here. Personally, I wish them well. Now think for a moment what the situation would have been like if Texaco didn't have an Omnsbud person, or even worse case scenario, she was white, even worse than that, if she was a white male. What do you think the results would have been? I'd bet you any amount of money they would have been extremely different My point is that unless we start strategically placing ourselves in positions to look out for each other, we are doomed. We are just modernized slaves. I'm not saying that the Omnsbud person did me any favors, all I am saying is that those racist bastards weren't even hearing anything I was trying to say. They didn't give a damn if I brought Jesus to Texaco. Now, if I were white, I would have been the greatest thing since apple pie and Chevrolet. My point again is that they look out for their interest, we need to look out for ours, and since we started from such a disadvantage because of slavery, we have to overcome many more obstacles. We can't just become a Texaco overnight, but we have to ensure that equality is there for us, and the only way to ensure that is through the people who represent us. That means the people in office, but even more than that, the people in the pulpits. We must hold them accountable for the political decisions that affect our race. Let me tell you, the same way every church you go to is saying turn to the person next to you in the pews and say neighbor, is the same way they can influence the decisions coming out of Washington D.C. If all the Black churches unite on one platform and hold those accountable for their decisions to build more prisons instead of more schools, and spend more money for war than for education, or our vote will go for someone who does want to build more schools and spend more on education, trust me, things will be a lot different. So why isn't this happening today? Someone is obviously selling us out again. With all the money/tithes being collected from the people in the churches, and you see the conditions that still plague our race, it just ain't adding up as far as I can see. Something is systemically wrong with our churches. The church used to be at the forefront of all our affairs, and any and all inequities encountered by our people. However, today, the church is status quo. So if you are poor and Black you are just out of luck. Let me ask you this one question. What do you think the ratio is of poor Blacks to rich Blacks? I'm going to venture and guess, twenty to one. So for every twenty thousand poor there are one thousand rich. I think that is probably a low estimate. I would dare to venture to say that for every one hundred poor Blacks there is one rich. That sounds a bit more accurate. So for every one hundred thousand poor there are one thousand rich. That's in America. What do you think the figure is in Africa? I dare not venture to guess, but I know as all know that it is some astronomical number, yet do you see anyone doing anything to change that. There isn't a damn thing going on in Africa comprehensively as a continent, five centuries after the fact. Again I point back to the lack of leadership. There is no one in the 21st century, no one. I surely don't see no Moses on the horizon, but you never know. I am convinced that due to the scope of the irreparable damage that has been caused by the *House Negro* over the centuries, specifically the last two generations, after the deaths of Malcolm and Martin, we have reached a point of no return. Because of this, the only solution that seems to be able to repair the irreparable is the Final Chapter, Revelations. It is going to take a major intervention to make right the wrong, and right now I don't see any other way. Even so, I believe that there is a reason why the Final Chapter is necessary, because until it's fulfilled, my people will continue to suffer disproportionately, universally, and the poor of the world will continue to increase continuously and exponentially. As I continuously critique events in society and how the world continues to undermine the Black Race like no other race, and with no voice still to represent the truth of the oppressiveness that we are subjected to, intervention by a Higher Authority is the only viable and logistical solution available. At present it is the only way. The Book must be fulfilled. It is actually the only basis of hope for us even if it is the end. It will be poetic justice when the rapture takes place. I guess that's why the hereafter is so appealing to us because the majority of us are still catching hell 'up in here'.

Chapter 10
The Takeover

There's gonna be weeping and gnashing of teeth. The Grim Reaper has now come to Texaco and it's gonna be a sad day for many, although there ain't that many of us left on this plantation anyway. It's mostly those in middle management that are catching the brute force of this storm. Given this new trend in Corporate America of downsizing and globalization, these middle management jobs have now become extinct. Never again will they make those exorbitant salaries they have come to know and enjoy at Texaco. The irony of this whole takeover is that Texaco used to be the major stakeholder of the Texaco/Chevron joint venture. Now Chevron is purchasing Texaco. Because of the arrogant disposition by the managers at Texaco towards the Chevron employees when Texaco was in charge, and how they used to abuse the employees of Chevron, now that Chevron was in control, boy oh boy, as they say in the hood, "payback is a bitch". And it was now payback time. The takeover could have went either way, but both companies knew that with the major consolidations transpiring, like Exxon/Mobil, and BP/Amoco, in order to even stay minutely competitive, something had to be done. Both had the money to acquire the other, but Chevron was a bit more pressed to make a deal by its Board than Texaco (according to an article that I read in the Wall Street Journal, you know, my Corporate Bible). I think Texaco used this opportunity to get out of the confines of the lawsuit and its requirements. With the takeover, Chevron didn't have to assume the liabilities Texaco had from the lawsuit. When you think about it, that was a great way to get rid of all their slaves. The CEO secured a position with the new company and was basically trying to secure the position as CEO. Eventually he ended up being escorted out of the building, however, he left well endowed. Soon I was going to have to leave the plantation, as they were escorting people out left and right. Since I was in Records, all the files had to be shipped from the entire Corporate Headquarters to the warehouse in Tulsa, Oklahoma. So basically, our department was slated to be one of the last ones to go. Personally, I was calculating how much money I could leave with if I stayed for X amount of months. I tossed and turned, and I'm telling you, a voice kept telling me to leave this sinking ship. I was still calculating figures and how much more money I could acquire if I stayed till the end of the year, which would mean four more weeks of vacation I could get paid for, and another year of severance to my time already served with the company. I was going crazy trying to figure it all out, and that voice kept ringing in my head saying leave now. So I cut the umbilical cord, pulled the plug and sent a memo to the Head of the Department, making sure that my sudden departure, in approximately one week would not affect my severance and that this was to remain strictly confidential. Let me tell you, it was the best feeling I had in a very long time. I felt like I had just took my life back. I was truly free! I mean it! I was free! "Free at last, Free at last, Thank God Almighty,

Free at last". I also left because I knew that they were getting ready to send down thousands upon thousands of boxes for shipment to Tulsa, and I said to myself that I was not going out like no slave. So I left the plantation. Throughout the company the news spread like wild fire, I didn't even tell my supervisor a thing. I just left. As far as I was concerned he didn't matter. It was like they were saying, how dare you leave on your own terms. It was like, you leave when we say leave. I wasn't about to wait to be escorted out, and the way things were going in Records, I think that I would have been fired because I wasn't about to do none of that work, shipping all those boxes. I basically said kiss off, all of you. That's when I realized that money is not more important than your dignity. I left with my dignity intact and in place. As for the crop of new *House Negro*es, they too were shocked. It didn't matter anymore, because I was through, and I had a legitimate out. I had met, fought, and conquered Goliath. All I knew was that I didn't ever want to have to do that again. Not only because it was so intense, but also because I never was intending to lay it all out like that again ever for a bunch of self-serving, parasitical, and useless people. I felt peace, serenity, and also empowered. Everybody was asking, do you have another job, what are you going to do? Where are you going to work? Hell, I didn't know, but all I knew was that I was leaving from that place. In the back of my mind was that saying by Malcolm X, that, "you are always in trouble when you have to rely upon your enemy for a job." Never once did I ever regret leaving that plantation. Not one time. I guess that is the fundamental difference between me and a *House Negro*. What's interesting was the fact that white people couldn't believe that they were being kicked off the plantation. I thought it was poetic justice. I was Zipping up my boots, going back to my roots. It was like being a soldier returning home from war, even though I've never been in the Armed Forces, but plenty of my family have, and still are. I had made a conscious decision not to ever return to Corporate. I'll also tell you, that there is no place like home, back to my people. When I took a look around, and as I reflected back to the Texaco years, I understood what has separated me from the *House Negro*. When I saw the love, felt the love from the people in my community, and people from my childhood, how they would greet me with such respect and admiration, it was really a tremendous feeling. I am sure proud of where I grew up, despite the negative stereotypes that is associated with living in the Projects. The city I grew up in was small, yet large enough to be categorized as a major city. Everyone knew everyone and people cared for each other. It was a real community and at present it is majority Black. It had its moments during the heroin epidemic of the fifties and sixties, and the crack epidemic of the eighties and nineties, but now Blacks have control of the City politically, and there are great things happening there. It is probably the most comprehensive example of what African villages were like when we ruled as kings and queens. Remember when I referenced the story of how I went to my homeboy's college and asked if there could ever be a successful revolution? Well my community is a living, breathing example of success, a Black Mayor who isn't afraid of whites, Blacks or anybody. Do you remember that old song by the Staple Singers, from back in the day called, 'I'll take you there'? Well that's what this City is like. I know a place, where people from all over the world have come to live, over ninety different nationalities. We're not the richest, but we're richer than most culturally. One thing for sure, ain't no smiling faces. You know those types of individuals that smile in your face. And there definitely ain't no room for no *House Negro*es. You may think that I am saying these things because it's my hometown and one day I might want to be Mayor, but I'm telling you, this Community is truly different from any other city in the country, maybe the world. It is a living breathing example of people who know who they are and treat others with respect and dignity. There are no boundaries, like in Corporate America, where they print the rhetoric and say we have policies and we are an equal opportunity employer, yet when you look at their Boardrooms, and when you look at their Cabinets, when you look at their management, it's so plain to see that the rhetoric says one thing, but what is really going on is so obvious. They are not trying to include us in any of it. When you look at sports and look in the stands, who do you see? When you look at who's playing, who do you see? When you look at the owners, who do you see? When you look at the coaches, who do you see? Yeah I know, we are making quote unquote, 'so-called progress', and inroads in coaching, but at the upper echelon of the industry who do you see? Who do you see? What's my point? My point is, for example, when you look at my hometown you know what, we don't have racial violence. Don't get me wrong, we do have some violence, but it ain't racially motivated. Now why is that? Yet, if you walk in some white neighborhoods in other communities like in NYC, you better be very damn careful. Why is that? It is because the Black leadership in our community is all about inclusiveness. Not just the rhetoric, and the speeches, but we live it. We as a city understand the importance of diversity, however, prior administrations didn't. Our City understands that when someone comes home from being incarcerated, they are going to need an opportunity for employment. Do you have any idea what that must be like? Hell no! Black or White, ain't nobody trying to give them an opportunity. I mention leadership because here is an example of Black leadership that works. I guarantee you that if some Uncle Tom *House Negro* walks up in the Mayor's office talking that bullshit about life on the plantation is good and *massa* ain't so bad, he will tell them to get the hell out of his office. Understanding the cancer that such mentality brings to any place, a city, a community, a school, any place, will ultimately destroy, and unless there is someone who understands the irreparable damage this mentality can cause we are surely doomed. Now you may understand why I speak so highly of my City. Not to mention the fact that we have many famous people who have come out of this City, professional basketball players, actors, and musicians. We have the distinct honor of having one of

Hollywood's greatest Black actors come out of our City. Even though I personally have left on occasion, I always come back home. I tell you all of this so you can begin to see how things could be, and are, when the *House Negro* is null and void. Just imagine for a moment if in my community, our Mayor was a *House Negro*. That major retail project consisting of Best Buy, Target, TJ Maxx, Bed Bath and Beyond and PETCO, would have never taken place because the white people in the town next door sued the City fifteen times to stop the project. If he were a weak, pathetic *House Negro*, he would have given in to the pressure being brought upon the city by these white people in the town next to us. However, he fought them to the end, and because of the retail sales revenue generated annually by this project, (to the tune of approximately five million dollars) the City is developing like never before. That's leadership, that's the difference between having these weak so-called leaders who supposedly represent us vs. having someone who will stand up for what is best for his people. I speak about this because when you look at the leadership of the Black American today, it is pathetic. People are only as good as their leadership. Because of the leadership in our City, we have a people who are proud to be Black. Imagine if we had representation like that throughout the nation. We used to, and it is becoming more and more obvious that now we don't. Nowhere in the entire state of New York can you find what we have in this City. Oh by the way, the city is Mount Vernon, otherwise known as 'Money Earnin Mount Vernon,' a phrase coined by "Heavy Dee" one of the famous rappers, of course, from our City. You can best believe that you can't find this in any other city in New York, and you probably won't find it anywhere else in the United States. You know, when I think about it, it's relatively simple. When you foster a cultural climate like that at Texaco which was arrogant, insensitive, negative and discriminatory, which by the way exist in most corporations, even today in the year 2007, eventually your demise is inevitable. People will one day rise up and fight against a system like that. Just like what's happening in this country today, and all over the world, but without strong leadership, ultimately these rebellions will disappear. They usually find a couple of guinea pigs to pay off, who will sell out their people and make a deal that is beneficial for themselves, for a minimal amount of power. I believe that is exactly what has happened to us, and that's where the *House Negro* comes in. Just for the record, the *House Negro* doesn't have to only be of the Black Race. He can be from any Race. It's anyone who sells his people out. It just seems most prevalent amongst us, probably because we are the most oppressed. Without our oppression many will fall. Hell, if we don't keep going to prison how the hell are they going to be able to maintain them, where will the contracts come from to build more prisons in those communities that don't have any other source of revenue? They damn sure don't build prisons in Black communities. Do you realize the millions and probably billions of dollars that are spent for the building of prisons which, of course, we have the distinct honor of occupying. Do you realize how many jobs would be lost without the prison population, of which we make up the majority. The oppressing of our race is necessary, unless they want to make the illegal immigrant felons, then they could have the distinct honor of being the new majority, not only as minorities, but also in prison. Right now, for all intents and purposes, it is easier to keep doing us, because we ain't got no-one around to legitimately challenge these genocidal practices being inflicted upon our race. That was part of the master plan. Don't you realize that when they plan, they plan for at least twenty-five years at a time. After they killed Malcolm and Martin things were going so well, they probably decided to go for another fifty years. Take a look around Black people, who is really representing us nearly forty years later? No one! I hear more coming from Blacks about immigration than I hear about the 58% unemployment of Black males in this country. What kind of leadership is that? I think in the last election more Blacks voted for Bush than in the first election that he outright stole. Now look at where we are. Idiots, just like back when they sold us into slavery. Nothing but those god damn *House Negro*es. Just because there are one or two people in positions, these *House Negro*es believe that those who have been against them are now for them. Same for the Hispanics, if the Republicans loved you so much, then why the hell is there so much controversy about letting you come here to live and work. Even if you're not educated, doesn't mean you have to be stupid. Look at where the majority of your people are and how they are living. If you're thriving and all around you, your people are dying, being killed, raped, robbed, enslaved, exploited, brutalized, and you are prospering, don't you think something's wrong, really wrong with that picture? If you don't, then something is really wrong with you, because this is what's going on all over the world. As people continue to flock over here, if they went through half of what we went through, they wouldn't want to come to this land of liberty and justice for all. What a hypocritical oath, as this country continues to do business with these dictators and tyrants, just like it did with South Africa while it was under Apartheid. Speaking of which, how was such a system able to come to fruition? How could a group of minorities just walk into Africa and take full control of an entire continent? Once again, I feel it necessary to reiterate that someone had to agree to this brutality. Someone had to sell out his people for whatever self-benefit. Someone was completely unmoved watching the total exploitation of his people. Someone had to guide them, someone who was a key figure, in order for this takeover to occur. Logistically, there isn't any other reasoning available to indicate otherwise. Just like the deal that the CEO made with Chevron. It was garbage. We the employees got royally screwed. Unless you had stock options, there was not much benefit in the takeover for the employees, especially the Blacks and minorities. My point is that the deal always comes from the top. Slavery was a deal that came from the top, Apartheid was a deal that came from the top, the Texaco settlement was a deal that came from the top. Whoever continues to negotiate for us is constantly selling us out. But just like it came, it can be taken apart by one individual who has the courage, like Mandela did against Apartheid. But how many Mandela's do we have vs. the *House Negro*es who constantly continue to sell us out. We have to fight our enemy and the *House Negro*. Maybe if we fight the *House Negro* first, then we would minimize a lot of the problems. Do you fight the drug dealer or the supplier to the drug dealer? As long as the supplier to the drug dealer is not being dealt with, the drug dealer will always be there. As long as the *House Negro* exists, we will always be sold out. Or should we confront the one who enables the *House Negro* to be a *House Negro*? So, do we get rid of the dealer or the supplier, the *House Negro* or the culprit? No *House Negro* no culprit, no dealer, no supplier, six of one, half dozen of the other. Take your pick. Before my experience in the discrimination lawsuit at Texaco, I would say kill all those racist bastards. After my experience with the Texaco lawsuit, I say kill all those worthless *House Negro*es. They disgust me more than any racist. Hell, you can be a racist, that's your damn business. But if you step to me the wrong way you best believe I'll break your neck. But the *House Negro* is a parasite. He is a cancer with no cure unless you treat it with extreme radiation to eradicate it. We need to eradicate ourselves of the *House Negro*. We didn't have to involve ourselves in the slave trade with the Portuguese. It may not be that simplistic, but when you break it down, it has to have an origin. It just didn't all of a sudden happen. It started someway, somewhere, somehow. Whether we want to face it is another story. To continue to blame others for what happened without acknowledging our role would be unrealistic and negligent. And you know all those who are the culprits love that! I can hear them now saying, yep, it wasn't our fault, why should we have to pay reparations. Hell, the Portuguese, who were one of the largest perpetrators in the slave trade, don't even have any money for reparations, they are too busy trying to come to America to do the slavery type work we once did. Poetic justice? Maybe! Do you know that millions of slaves went through Brazil? Rio de Janeiro to be exact. As we forge ahead on the reparations issue, I think we should also forge ahead and trace back to the ones who sold us in the first place and make their families pay reparations also. After all, they were the ones who participated in this brutal and barbaric trade. Those traitorous perpetrators, who conspired with these intruders and caused our demise. I guess some may say you need to let it go, you hear that often from the benefactors of the slave trade. It wasn't me, it was my ancestors. Imagine if they used that for an excuse for those persecuted by the Nazis. Even with the horror of slavery we are expected not to remember, because it makes them feel so uncomfortable. I say to hell with them and their uncomfortability. Like 9/11, we will never forget! And just like you want restitution, we want restitution. Bet they don't like that. I can hear them saying, and we thought he was a good *nigga*. How dare he compare slavery to the Holocaust? How can he even think of mentioning 9/11 in the same breath and the same scope as slavery? Actually, there is no comparison. Slavery was ten times worse than them both put together. Yet we as a group of people are expected to let it go! Get over it as they say. Why are we supposed to always turn the other cheek, and forgive all the ills that have fallen upon us by your hands? Actually, when studying the African Slave trade, the whole damn world is guilty. The whole damn world owes us restitution. So what is the price of restitution? What can the world even begin to do to correct the ills of the African Slave trade, the origin of crimes against humanity suffered by the Black Race? They stripped us of our identity, they forced our women, they forced their religion upon us and the Catholic Church did nothing regarding slavery. They actually felt that if we were baptized we would at least be saved in the after life. Actually, Bishops owned slaves also. Someone is going to burn in hell come Judgment Day. At least in Egypt, the Israelites were able to worship their God. You just had to give us your names too. I'll never forget that scene in 'Roots' the movie, when the slave master whipped the shit out of Kunta because he wanted him to say his name is Toby. At least the Hebrews were able to keep their names. Have you ever known an African named Peter? Someone needs to pay for these crimes. Until someone is held accountable for these crimes, we will never get the respect we are entitled to as human beings. Unless justice is served, it will always be just us. Something has to be done to eradicate this catastrophe. But when the whole World is the perpetrator of this crime against humanity, how do we put the whole world on trial? We probably would end up with some Black *House Negro* for an attorney, who might just end up negotiating us back into slavery. What's ironic is that after all of that, they still aren't tired of oppressing us. They camouflage their repressive tactics under the guise of equal opportunity employer. What a joke that is. Equal opportunity for the positions that they let the peasants fight over. They actually believe that bullshit because that's all it really is. Until you have actually been through one of these corporations and have experienced their discriminatory practices, you probably won't believe it. Most whites don't, because they never experience it, except maybe in the sixties and early seventies, when affirmative action was allowing us the opportunity for preferential treatment for positions in the corporation. Those damn white boys were having a fit, screaming reverse discrimination. The nerve of those bastards. That is why they need to pay reparations. They never want to see us succeed. That is why, when the takeover by Chevron occurred and most of those white people were about to lose their jobs and would probably never find another job paying like that, I was not feeling any sympathy for them at all. For us, we didn't have much of anything on the plantation anyway but you still had those who were scared to leave the plantation. Just sitting there, waiting for *massa* to say you gotta go now. That 's another reason why I left when I did. I was not about to let them have the satisfaction of escorting me off of the plantation. That really would have been the talk of the company. All those scared employees sitting on death row waiting for their execution date. For me, it was a new start. To where, I didn't know, but I knew a new life was about to begin. Hell, take a look at me now. I am light years from where I was after twelve years at Texaco. If you saw my wall in my office now, and the training that I've been through post Texaco, Texaco is totally meaningless, a pure waste of time, except for the lawsuit. When the takeover was announced many people in the company, Black and White, were ecstatic. People were tired of the sensitivity classes and the diversity and inclusiveness that had become the new buzz words for the organization. Zero tolerance was killing those racists. No more ethnic jokes. Many times, whites felt they could come up to me and say racial jokes. I am not sure why, but they did. Did I look like a *House Negro* to them? What was it that made them think that it was alright to say things like that to me? In any case, zero tolerance was about to remedy all of that. It was truly poetic justice in the grand scheme of things, considering that the fall of Texaco was imminent. The great Babylon has fallen, as they say in the Book of Revelations. The great Texaco has succumbed to all its evil, along with the destruction of the Rain Forest in Brazil, in which they denied any wrongdoing. If you knew Texaco like I did, you knew they were guilty of destroying the Rain Forest. Till the end they denied the damage they manufactured in the Rain forest. They knew damn well they left that place in ruins. Just like in the Chemical facility in Beacon, New York. That place was so polluted, that the water wasn't even consumable. They dumped so much chemical in the creek that the land was contaminated, so they tried to sell the buildings, because no one was willing to clean up the toxic mess.

You know if they did it here at home, you know they did it abroad. They had no regard for the environment, like many other major oil companies. They pay off the *House Negro*es, and Politicians and call it a day. It was good to see Texaco destroyed. The lawsuit with Getty, just another example of the arrogance, the racial discrimination lawsuit, again no wrongdoing, they paid their way out of everything, but it finally caught up to them. Hopefully this will be a message to all the other corporations who continue to abuse their power, like Enron and MCI. I remember when I used to work temp at MCI and right before Christmas they laid off an entire building. I was saying to myself, they have no class. Now look at them. As a business major I just felt as though that was really bad business. What I didn't understand, and still don't understand, is why is it so difficult for these companies to incorporate good business practices. They are so entrenched in their modus operandi that good business and good business ideas are simply shot down, ultimately at the expense of the organization. That is exactly why I say, because of this mentality, we are losing in this global business economy. We are in debt to China to the tune of, last time I read the Wall Street Journal, two hundred and two billion dollars. Now that's outright ridiculous. I'm telling you, if someone doesn't open their eyes soon we are no longer going to be the leading economic power. I guess as long as we are the sole military power nothing else matters. Sounds a little like the Roman Empire. We all know what happened to them. The fall of America? I don't know what to think of this country without the American

Dream. Even I believed in the American Dream at one time. However, can you begin to imagine what those crazies might do without the American Dream? We saw what they did during the depression! I wouldn't be surprised if they pushed the button, from up in the space shuttle of course. Especially when you consider all the activity going on in those space stations up there. If you think that this is so far fetched, then why do you think Congress was going crazy over the thought that China was proposing to buy a U.S. Oil Company, I believe, Conoco Oil, yet they initially approved the sale of our major ports to Dubai. In other words, you can blow up our Country, but don't mess with our oil. I'm telling you, these Good Ole Boys are mad! They are insane! If things keep going in the direction that they are, we won't even be around for Revelations. I'm telling you that they will destroy the whole world themselves. You first must realize that this is the most powerful nation on earth, and leaning real close to the characteristics of an Empire. George wants to be king, like his Arab buddies in the Middle East. No matter how much power George thinks he has, he still has to get permission, even though he tries to bypass Congress. Even his Republican counterparts are questioning his tactics. His boys in the Middle East give a directive and no one is allowed to question it. I mean, if all my boys were kings I definitely would want to experience what that feels like. It's only human nature. I know he is saying boy oh boy, I sure wish I didn't have to go through that damn democratic process. By no means am I saying that democracy, when practiced, is not a good thing, however, how much of it are we really practicing over here? I remember one of my college professors saying that inevitably we will begin to see a shift in democracy, where democracy becomes more communistic, and communism becomes more democratized. I thought he was nuts back then, but now when you look at where we are as a society and the impact that 9/11 has had upon our nation and the Patriot Act, there is actually some validity to his theory. There is no question that Big Brother is watching, and he needs to, however by watching to this degree, certain inalienable rights have to be forfeited. That's just the facts. Like it or not it is what it is. So where are we, and where do we go from this point forward? You know in Asia they are teaching the decline of the American Empire and the new beginning of theirs. Again I must point out the new economic power that China has ascertained. And believe me, we are in no kind of position to tell China they need to be more democratic. It ain't gonna happen and ain't about to happen. For those of you who are not aware, China is a Communist State with a terrible Human Rights record, but if I'm not mistaken, good ole President Bill pushed for them to have most favored nation status in the United Nations. The tables are shifting and we better be very careful as a Nation. As a Black man in this Country what can I really say, knowing the truth and continually learning more truths. It's almost like watching the demise of Texaco. I say this because this Country has been, and continues to be, anti Black in all of its policies, both from the Democratic and Republican Parties. Until you whites realize that there is a direct correlation between our success and your success, and conversely our failure and your failure, this Country will fall, just like Texaco, which was once a tremendous symbol of and for America. You continue, both corporately and politically, to choose not to do right by us. Slowly but surely the paradigm of power is shifting. Slowly but surely other nations are beginning to rise up and challenge you. I say this because you continue to exclude us from the equation. Even though many went to fight with the British in the Revolutionary war, it was the Black soldier that helped America win the war. Conversely, you used the draft in the Vietnam War, Blacks, especially after Muhammed Ali chose not to fight in the war, were inspired to denounce the draft and not fight in that war because of this Country's racist policies towards us here in America, and guess what? America definitely did not succeed in Vietnam, actually you got your asses kicked in that war. What am I saying? I am saying that without us, this Country would not exist. Surely we would be speaking German or Japanese right now. We are the key to America's success. We are the key to the world's success. Together, just like when King spoke at the Washington Monument, he saw it, he understood it. Together, we could build a world that was as pleasing to God as the temple Solomon built. America could have been that shining example for the world to see and desire to replicate. America could have brought new meaning to the Pledge of Allegiance, America the Beautiful, My Country tis of Thee. Other Countries have to look at the Black man and ask how in the world can he say the Pledge of Allegiance and sing those songs, when collectively America still oppresses him, and treats him like shit! To the rest of the world, they probably think we are as dumb as America portrays us to be, like back in those Tarzan movies. We ain't gonna never overcome, yet we have overcome many of the obstacles that you have put in our way toward freedom, yet somehow, another barrier of entry is continually created to plague us. Is it because you really think we are idiots, because we fell for your deception and treachery, as did the Indians? Or is it because after all the abuse, the deceit, and brutality, we believe in this system called the American way? An outsider looking in, psychoanalyzing this, maybe after all is said and done, as we study civilizations today, when they look back at how we were abused in America and by America, truly they will have to wonder why we fought so hard to be part of a society that didn't want us, and only conceded because of the brutality inflicted upon us publicly to the world during the Civil Rights Movement. So I am asking my people, here and now, are we idiots, or fools, to continue to believe in this system? I say no, we are neither because this system holds the key and potential to such greatness. I say we are idiots for believing in those who continue to promise us the key to this potential, and that's where the *House Negro* comes in. Example, the *House Negro* says I made it so why can't everyone else? It amazes me how a Black person can make it all the way to the Supreme Court of this land that is soaked with the blood of his people and turn around and denounce the same legislation that allowed him to get to where he is. Does he not think that if it wasn't

216

for the Civil Rights Movement, that he would have ever had such an opportunity? What damn school would he have been able to attend to get the necessary education? Surely Brown vs. the Board of Education afforded him the opportunity. Damn sure wouldn't have been able to attend Harvard! Verily, verily I say unto thee, are you 'blind and do not see'? "What profiteth a man if he should gain the whole world and lose his soul". The *House Negro* has sold his soul. And I don't mean his ability to dance. It was those same kind of idiots that sold us into bondage. His associates have to look at him and say what a loser. Surely they would never sell out their people like that. That is why they look at us the way they do. How can you blame them? Same thing with the Chairman of the Diversity Task Force at Texaco who, one year later, became General Counsel. It was achieved on the backs of his own people who suffered in that systemic racist corporation. No sense of pride and/or dignity. Sell your soul Black man, sell your soul Black woman. I know whites are having a field day with that behind closed doors. They just make sure no one has a tape recorder to hear what they really think of those *House Negro*es who sell us out everyday of the week here in this Country. What a sad testament to a people who were once Kings and Queens. Like with the Texaco tapes, where they were calling us *niggas*, black jellybeans, porch monkeys and only they know what else, sense we never got the opportunity to hear what the tapes said in its entirety. I guess the *House Negro* doesn't think that they could have possibly been talking about him. After all, they boast about the schools they have attended, and the many Boards that want them to join. Well, just for the record *House Negro*, they were calling you a *nigga* too. How can you possibly believe that they are distinguishing you from me *House Nigga?* This is why I am totally convinced that Blacks in the future are in serious jeopardy. Not so much because of the subversive tactics employed upon us by our enemies, but by the same mentality of our own kind, which sold us, (that's right, 'sold' is the operative word here) into slavery. It's the same mentality of those who sold us then, who are selling us out now, down the path of genocide today. Realistically, who are our examples of leadership in this nation? What individual can our youth look up to and say they want to emulate when they grow up, other than rappers, basketball players and T.V. or movie stars? Yes, to a certain degree that is all our youth are more readily exposed to, but who is making sure that they are aware of the great accomplishments that have taken place since our enslavement in this Country? I remember receiving an e-mail that had all the inventions that we created in and for this Country. How come our children don't have that as part of their curriculum? Actually, I myself, who considers himself highly educated, a scholar and intellect, had no idea that we invented all these firsts in this Country for its development during the Industrial Revolution. And I 'm a grown man. What is wrong with that picture? I studied history at the collegiate level, yet I didn't know a damn thing about what we did. Our history is totally excluded from America, and this has got to change. No longer can this bullshit being taught as history be accepted. Someone should be fighting for the contribution of our race to be included in the educational process. Guess what? I think I have found a new purpose! If all goes as planned with the writing of this book, I will personally take up the banner and fight for this knowledge and information of our Race and it's accomplishments and contributions to become part of a nationwide curriculum. Not just to be conveyed during Black History Month, but as basic as learning the alphabet and addition. It is time we take our rightful place in history, past, present and the future, if there is such a thing as future history. This would actually instill a real sense of pride in our youth to know that, not only before slavery, but during, and after slavery, against all odds, we still managed to emerge victorious, because we are and always were a great people. Imagine that, the snowball effect of highlighting the enormous contributions that have been made in America by our people, taught throughout all schools as part of American History. I am not suggesting, teaching the brutality of slavery, which is already well documented, but focusing on the positive life-changing inventions that have made this Country great. Hell, even the *House Negro* would be able to stop being ashamed of his heritage. You know, I actually believe this could work. A legitimate solution to our internal problems; the only obstacle I foresee is getting this passed as a curriculum course. Somehow, I perceive that teaching this may be as difficult as the battle ensuing about 'intelligent design'. Maybe this could become a venue for those pathetic individuals perpetrating like leaders, to legitimately have a worthwhile non-combatant, non-violent, highly educational platform to stand on without getting a bullet in their head. Just remember that I thought of it first. I know, the nerve of me wanting to take credit for an idea that might save my people and allow us non-threateningly to take our rightful place in the world. Truth is, there isn't any other race, White, Spanish, Native American, Asian, or any other that I may have left out, or that you may want to throw into the equation, that has contributed more to the development of this society as a whole than us. If you can show me a group who has, let me know, and I will be more than happy to retract this statement. I know you're saying, there go those damn Negroes again talking about the great civilizations they used to have before we came and raped, killed, and stole their culture from them, and talking about those damn pyramids that we still can't figure out how to build. How were they built? Oh, don't forget that garbage about Cleopatra being Black. 'Now where the hell did they get that from'? 'Didn't they see the movie'? 'Don't they know that Elizabeth Taylor is Cleopatra'?

As I embark upon the idea of bringing this knowledge to light, somewhere in my mind I can hear the voice of the EEOC at Texaco saying, now don't be going around here talking about you got a degree. Well if they ain't recognizing me for my work ethic, then what the hell else am I supposed to do? While we continue to languish in this educational system, and since education is the true key to success, then it only makes sense to incorporate into the curriculum of education the true history of Blacks in America. OK, maybe not the whole history because there are some areas that would implicate this Country in such a negative way from all the white lies, that it would do more harm than any good in the field of education. Some may argue, and probably will argue, that they don't want their children learning anything good about the Black Race. It would be foolish not to anticipate such reactions from a society that has portrayed us in such a negative manner. I still submit that this could be the catalyst to change much of the negative stereotypes and misconceptions that we encounter on a daily basis. "I have a dream" but this ain't no dream, this is something that is necessary for the continuance of our nation if we are to emerge as a truly great nation. If you don't believe me, just wait and see what happens if we continue going in the direction we are going.

Chapter 11
It's Over It's Done

The reality of no longer being employed at Texaco is now final. My new birth had begun, and I must admit, it was a bit scary. The unknown, and the reality pertaining to future employment, especially here in the County of Westchester, knowing that I played a part in the destruction of this organization, was a very serious thing. Yeah, I felt proud about it, but now the reality about future employment, not only as a Black Man, but an African American formerly employed at an organization that was faced with a racial discrimination lawsuit was now beginning to loom large. The other reality was that when constructing my new resume, I realized that for twelve years I hadn't accomplished much of anything. Basically, I was just about where I had started when I first came to Texaco. I had no real career path, and I wasn't trying to be a bean counter again. Sure, I trained people, and learned a new computerized accounting system, but I did that, years before I ever reached Texaco. Other than the Community Relations work that I did, and did well, I may add, there was nothing significant about my growth on paper that would really make anyone want to hire me, especially after the lawsuit. I will say this, however, never once did I desire to return back to the plantation, not once. I remember a Black female employee who returned as a temp to be a receptionist. She was telling me how difficult it was out there trying to find employment, especially after they found out you were a former

Texaco employee. Previously, she worked in Investors Relations, the department that I had my first interview with when I arrived at Texaco as a Temp. That interview was for a data entry clerk. During the interview it wasn't difficult to see that we had different ideas pertaining to the position. They wanted someone who was going to be a career data entry clerk, while I was asking questions pertaining to upward mobility and career development. That should have been my first clue about the mentality that was prevalent at Texaco. I know they wouldn't have asked a white boy with a degree if he wanted a career as a data entry clerk. The fact that they would even suggest that to me knowing I had a degree was insulting in itself. What was it that made them have the gall to think that I would want to be a data entry clerk forever? That was their mentality. Needless to say, I didn't get the job. Later, as I began my new career delivering boxes, I would run into the two gentlemen who interviewed me. As I became familiar with the department and certain policies of that department, I was glad that I didn't work in that prison camp they had going on in there.

Many became victims after they left Texaco, simply because they didn't have any marketable skills. You must remember that most Blacks who were at Headquarters were in menial positions. I myself, even with a degree, had no real developmental or marketable skills after twelve years with the company. Imagine those who had been there twenty and twenty five years! The reality of this situation was coming home fast and I really needed to figure out what the hell I was going to do. Since I had decided that I wasn't ever going back to corporate again, coupled with the fact that corporate probably would never hire me again, I was steadfast that I wasn't going back to the plantation.   You see there is an inherent difference between the *House* and Field Negro, as Malcolm would say. In this case at Texaco there were those who feared the worst when Texaco was going down, especially the whites. However, there shouldn't have been one Black that should have given a damn about Texaco shutting down. But just like back on the plantation when *massa* came to many of them after the Civil War saying, "I can't pay you much but if you stay and work the farm I will pay you what I can and give you food." Just like out in the Desert with Moses, when Dathan convinced many that they were better under the taskmaster's whip in Egypt than out in the Desert following Moses. What makes one man say no, never again, and another man remain or accept slavery and oppression? Do I dare venture to say that it may be genetic? I do know for a fact that it comes from within your heart and deep from inside your soul. Is it innate? I am even more convinced than ever that it is inherited. How could one be OK with his children growing up a slave, where another would do everything, even give his life to make sure that his family would not have to be subjected to the perils of such brutality. I mean, you can go around singing 'we shall overcome' and maybe it becomes a self-fulfilling prophecy, but unless you take a stand and say that you ain't taking it no more, it may take four hundred more years. I submit that the child learns from the parent and if the parent is docile then the child in all likelihood will be docile. Conversely, the same applies. If the child sees the parent stand up for truth and justice and the American way, well maybe not the American way, but truth and justice, then he too will more than likely stand up for truth and justice. It's really a fundamental difference, a shameful fundamental difference. For example, when the King sells his people to be slaves and the heir apparent watches this, in all likelihood the son will do the same as his father. It's that simple, dangerous but simple. This is why I submit that the *House Negro* and the Leaders in Africa and our so-called self-proclaimed leaders today, have inflicted irreparable damage upon its people. If you look at some of the trades that were made with the white man by the tribal leaders of Africa, you would have to think that these were some "dumb ass *niggas*". I know, what language, well I guess it's better than calling them "*stupid ass motha- fuckas*". They are the ones who are responsible for our demise. It was the white man that was responsible for the brutality of our people. Again, don't forget, the Portuguese were the initial perpetrators in this business. Havana, Cuba was a large player. Sugar was the motivation to go deeper into Africa and seek the darker, stronger slave because the other slaves, Indians, Spanish, couldn't do the labor. I hate sugar cane! No wonder it gives us diabetes. We should hate it. It expedited our captivity. Ask me, we should boycott sugar all together. With the discovery of sugar, the demand became so strong that there weren't enough slaves to keep up with the demand. Spain emerged as one of the most powerful empires and fell once it could no longer get the required amount of slaves to continue the production of the sugar cane crop. You must remember, it was an agricultural society at that time. There were forts built in Africa, and battles fought by different factions like the Dutch, German, French, and English for slaves. They basically kicked the Spanish out of business. That is why I said damn near the whole world would have to make restitution to us for slavery. Don't forget the Catholic Church is guilty also. What is sad, is that even after all of this, after Martin and Malcolm and those before, and the fact that there hasn't been any after, we are still trapped, even in the 21st century. It has got to end. I am hoping, with the revalidation of my People in history, that maybe there is some hope left for us. However, if the revalidation of my People does not manifest, I'm afraid that it will ultimately result in the necessity of the separation of the wheat from the tare, as the ultimate fulfillment that The Book of Revelations has prophesied. I guess by any means necessary. I guess it's an appeal to God, like in the time of Sodom and Gomorrah, when God would spare the City if he could find one righteous person. I'm wondering if we could find one righteous cause, maybe the Lord would spare us the ultimate Rapture. Or is the Rapture the only righteous solution? This wrong must be righted, and if not, I feel the consequences are and will be grave. Can a fundamental difference be the cause for such a catastrophic end? Well, how about this for an example. I give you the Roman Empire! Surely they thought they would rule forever. I also give to you the British Empire! They colonized the world. Surely they thought they would crush the rebellion of America. The irony of this is, the only reason Britain exist today is because of its alliance and its pledge of allegiance to America. The crown is bogus and the Queen is now nothing more than a figurehead! So be very careful! Be very, very careful, cause judgment awaits all!

I guess it's like, "he who hath wisdom let him hear". Imagine history if Moses never was. What was that fundamental characteristic of Moses, even when he was considered Egyptian? What was that fundamental force that made him choose and acknowledge his heritage, while the people who were from the Islands put down "other" until they found out that the lawsuit was for Blacks only? Only then they became Black and real damn fast may I add. *Bastards*! Don't like what I'm saying, well don't get mad at me for telling the truth. It's people like you who confirm exactly what I am saying about the opportunistic, useless *House Negro*. That is why it is imperative that we rid our Race of these useless bastards. They are parasitical and will suck the life out of any and everything. Are you now beginning to see and understand the irreparable damage that manifests when one undermines who they really are vs. one who stands up for who they are, and what's right? In this case it wasn't even a matter of standing up, because it was their option and they thought it would be more beneficial to disassociate themselves from being classified as Black. All that is, is the shame, degradation, inferiority, and lack of understanding of how important it is to be proud of who you are. I can't think of any other race in this world that is ashamed of who they are and where they come from. Now if the history of Blacks were to become accepted in society, it would enable those who are ashamed of being Black, to hold their heads up. That's all that's at stake here. The ability to hold your head up vs. walking around feeling that being Black is detrimental to your existence and diminishes your opportunity to share in the American Dream. These are the reasons why I feel that unless we derive some other methodology and strategy, we as a people will be lost forever. Personally, I've never been an advocate of marching, and I think that we, not anyone else but us, need to stop thinking that the only solution every time something goes wrong is to get together and go a marching. You *House Negro*es are so brainwashed you can't even think of something different. You don't even use the pulpit, except to convince people of how they need to tithe. Why don't you speak about how we are going to continue to fight until schools throughout this nation teach about us in the development of this nation and the world, again, not so much as to expose all the ills of slavery, but about the new renaissance of education in our educational system. The inclusion of us, the incorporation of us, in spite of all that has happened to us. That's not a crime, is it? No Child Left Behind is a travesty and that is being pushed all over the Country. Hell, everywhere you go to church or look on TV, you hear them saying the same damn thing, look at your neighbor and say neighbor, and then whatever, and everyone says it. Well let's look at our neighbor and say neighbor, it's time for the truth to be taught. Not just for us to know, cause God surely knows we don't have a clue, but for all to know. Yeah, I know it might make the Nazi's mad and the Ku Klux Klan mad, and they might require equal time to teach about their heritage and history and what they have contributed to society, and this great nation, and they should be able to do just that. Lets' look and see briefly what they have contributed, other than bloodshed and the brutalization of a race of people. What did they create except machinery for war? although German engineering is awesome. Ok that's one. I am really going to need some help with this. Fact is, there isn't much there, especially when compared to us. I mean, let's put it to the test. Let's take any race, put them side by side with the Black Race and do a comparative analysis of their contributions to society. For the most part, there ain't nothing but blood on their hands. I'm telling you, there isn't any Race that can stand up next to ours, yet we lack the knowledge of what we have accomplished. Regardless of the fact that we fill the prisons, in spite of the fact that we remain the highest unemployed, we still manage, and have always managed, to rise. However, I fear that we are running out of chances and time. I know certain groups of people are going to look at this and say where the hell does he get off? I can hear them saying that *nigga* is crazy. Who the hell wants to hear that nonsense, like Blacks are superior or something? Actually, I am not saying any of that. But if we were not, then why did you have to spend so much time destroying everything we represented? Yet, I am not asking that they teach that as part of the curriculum. It is amazing, however, that Blacks have managed to, and continue to survive, even though they have been barbarically and viciously oppressed. All I am suggesting is that in America, they teach about the inventions and inventors of our Race, to give all the opportunity to learn first hand, how we shaped and built this great Country. Something has to be done to help those pathetic low esteemed *House Negro*es. Understand this, if nothing else, when I refer to those pathetic, low esteemed, it isn't directed at those who are economically or socially oppressed, because amongst those individuals there is a fire that burns deeply against the treachery and the abuse they continue to suffer from in this Country. When they rebel with wreck less abandon, our so-called leaders of the Black Race can't even identify with it. I will say this, that within their anger there is a virtuosity that has kept us alive through all the abuse and the oppression. That is the group that they focus on, to oppress, because the so-called Black Leaders have lost touch with the fire that burns within those most oppressed. The Black leaders are even afraid of them. I myself, take great pride in the fact that I can still communicate with them. Actually, before I left the plantation, my plight wasn't that much different from theirs. I was living just enough. Not even paycheck to paycheck. I needed that next paycheck as soon as I got the first one. What is really interesting, and more so ironic, is the fact that now that I work in a Black Administration, I am no longer living just enough. I am not making more money than I was at Texaco, per se, however the support level is the difference. If you were to look at where I was in Texaco and where I am now, for the approximately two and a half years that I have been employed in the Black administration vs. the twelve years with Texaco, there is absolutely no comparison whatsoever. I am light years away from where I was. It's Incredible! It's Unbelievable! The training alone that I have received, which has allowed me to reach a level of respectability in a profession dominated by white males, is only through the support from this Black administration. I am respected by Police Chiefs, Fire Chiefs, Managers, Commissioners, Elected, and Appointed officials in administrations and in School Districts, as one with great insight in this field. Not so much because of me, but because of the support, that has been afforded to me. Two and a half years vs. twelve. I can proudly say that I am so damn glad that I left that plantation. Sure the road was a little bumpy at times, but I made some tremendous firsts after I left the plantation. Yeah, doing their garbage, their meaningless work, wasting away, yet walking around in my suit like I was someone important. Some people actually thought I was. You should have seen the look on many of their faces when they found out what area, or should I say the meaninglessness of the department in the corporation I represented. I looked the part, played the part, but never got the part, and with twelve years of nothing solid and some Office Assistant 3 as my status, what future was waiting for me after I left there? Nothing at all, not a damn thing! Lets forget about me, because I still had a degree, and no matter how hard they tried to minimize it, they could never take it away. Those individuals who didn't have more than high school and maybe one or two years of college were going to suffer a far worse fate than mine. Today I am not even sure where many of them are, or if they have safely landed professionally on another modernized plantation.

Interestingly though, is the fact that many of the whites in strategic positions, especially in the Corporate Services Department, didn't even have a degree. They were scared to death of what was about to happen to them out there in this bear market, especially since they weren't qualified for supervisory positions. Now they would have to go to an organization where the requirements for such a position would require a degree. Talk about 'chickens coming home to roost'. The reality of life after Texaco was going to be far more difficult for them than it was for us. Personally, I felt sorry for them. Not! And Chevron was about to exact revenge on all those who used to be Texaco employees who were now begging for jobs with them. Talk about poetic justice!

Want to know what's even more interesting? From the time that I graduated from college, to the point in my life after Texaco, approximately twenty years, (1980-2001), I was looking for that opportunity in Corporate America. Nothing ever emerged in all those twenty-one years. Yeah, I had jobs, for the most part, which I was over qualified for and would end up eventually quitting, but it was always entry-level positions that I was offered. I remember working in a bank, and for the record, I hate banks. They are some of the biggest crooks I have ever seen, but I remember them insisting that you must start out at the entry-level position as a teller, then, grow from there. I remember sitting at my teller station and watching the newly graduated white boy go straight upstairs to the Commercial Lending Department. I was wondering what happened to the bank policy of starting out from an entry-level position. Actually, that was an entry-level position, just not a position for a newly graduated colored boy like me. It was only as I sought employment, that I realized that the color of my skin had everything to do with the positions I would ascertain, compounded by the beginning of the Reagan-Years, where there was a backlash from White America about all the progress Blacks were making in the Corporate world. All of a sudden whites were screaming discrimination because Blacks were finally getting preferential treatment and access to the pie. We were making strides by leaps and bounds. We were exemplifying, that given a fair opportunity we could be great. When Black men were getting the jobs that were usually dedicated to white males and were becoming their superiors at work, they couldn't take it. They probably should have went to work for Texaco because that was never ever going to be a problem there. Well, Good Ole Boy Ronnie came riding in with his John Wayne mentality and began the dismantling of anything that the government had put in place for the development of Blacks. Why do you think that white folks believe that Ronald Reagan was one of the best Presidents ever? Now how the *fuck* could that be possible, when he was running the White House and had Alzheimer's. Now correct me if I'm wrong, but how in the world, if you have Alzheimer's, can you run the United States of America? Shit, my aunt just recently died having that shit, and I tell you it's no joke! When he died you would think that Jesus himself was being buried. Those eight years with him as President were probably the worst years that Blacks had ever experienced in America, compounded by the four more years with the first George Bush as president. Yeah that's right I said it! Twenty-one years on the corporate plantation, twelve under the regime of a Republican presidency and a backlash of white resentment to Blacks and Affirmative Action, which we all know is a curse word today. I graduated in time from college, however it was probably the worst time ever to seek employment as a Black male.

I know without a doubt, that when I left Texaco I felt the chains and the shackles fall off my back and ankles. I know you are probably wondering how can I say that? Just because they don't use the physical chains anymore does not mean that the chains aren't there. Even I felt the chains. What's interesting is, I thought that I was free and in control of my destiny. However, when I officially left, they fell off! I ain't lying, they really did! Those chains weren't just restricted to us, they were on everyone there. I knew that it was going to be a long and winding road ahead of me, but I was free! They also ain't lying when they tell you freedom isn't free, but it sure is a damn good feeling. You really have to try it at least one time in your life *House Negro*, preferably before you die. Once you try it, you will never accept anything else. One other note, just for equal time sake, per se, the last eight years in Corporate for me were under a Democratic presidency, Bill Clinton to be exact. I still can't figure out why Black people love Bill so much. I think we just have a history of following the wrong people. Just like the Jonestown massacre. A whole bunch a Black people followed this white preacher to the Promised Land and after they got there he eventually killed them or forced them to commit suicide by drinking poisoned kool-aid, men women and children. It is almost like that white man who came into Africa with the Bible in his hand and we ended up with Christianity and they ended up with our land. Ain't no difference because both were murderers. Idiots followed him all the way to Guyana. We loved Bill so much we didn't care what he did. I had a Black woman tell me "don't mess with Bill." I was like damn! Preachers even rationalized his infidelity. Personally, I ain't mad at him about that either, considering some of my escapades in the office with women, however, some of the legislation under his presidency really screwed Black people. My point is that if a Black person really believes that a white person from Arkansas is going to help them, they are in real serious trouble. I mean, just because he was on Arsenio Hall's TV show and played the saxophone, he was "our president." Those ignorant Blacks. I bet if you ask a Black person, why they like him, I bet you they couldn't give you a good reason why they voted for him, except he was a Democrat. We really need to rethink that also. So they stole our land with the Bible in their hand, and then we followed Jim Jones all the way to Guyana, how stupid is that Black people. Maybe it's because they had such a low level of self-esteem they followed him. Hopefully, in my quest to provide some information that would enhance my people's self esteem, and increase their level of understanding as to the accomplishments that have been achieved by us, maybe they will stop following white strangers and making asinine trades and selling their own people out.

Understand this if you will, and I guarantee this can stand up to any challenge. America said, give me your tired, your hungry and your poor, and they fled from their impoverished existence from abroad by the millions to come to America. Right? Right! This was based on the American Industrial Revolution. Right? Right! In the following chapter I will enclose all the inventions by African Americans that contributed to the American Industrial Revolution. I will even go as far as to say that without these inventions there would not have been an American Industrial Revolution, therefore eliminating the possibility for these poor impoverished whites to flee from their poverty. Make no mistake why they came here. They were living in horrible, unbearable conditions in their homeland. They came here with nothing. Why? Because they had nothing. If they had so much they wouldn't have had to come here. Right? So read very carefully my people and read very carefully white people, because you should be on your knees thanking us for saving your white ass from the poverty and despair you were living in before you came here during the American Industrial Revolution. Remember, if it wasn't for us, there would have never been anything close to the American Industrial Revolution, and we probably would have lost the war, and would be speaking German right now. You ought to be down on your knees thanking us! So next time an African American comes in looking for a job, think twice! Believe it or not, your future depends on it as much as it depended on you escaping the poverty from the origins of your birth! Take heed! 'He who hath wisdom let him hear!' I fear this prophecy will fall upon deaf ears. Yet I hope not, pray not!

Chapter 12

Black Inventors/ Black Inventions:

The New Curriculum

How can anyone dare fix their face to say that we, (African Americans), or whatever, Negroes, Colored, were not the ones who made the Industrial Revolution possible through our inventions. It is in black and white for all to see right here in this chapter 'Black Inventors/Black Inventions'. As I debated where to place this information, beginning, middle or end, for the fear that it may not get read, I challenge all who read this, to probe The Patent Process and Black Inventors of America, accompanied by two other documents from web sites of Black Inventors and Inventions. It's phenomenal, and undeniable, especially when you consider the time period in America with its racist, segregationalist policies and practices, it's amazing how we managed to even get patents, without the white man stealing that also, even though I am certain that there is a more detailed and comprehensive listing of our inventions. So are you ready for the New Curriculum, the National Educational Initiative (NEI) featuring Black Inventions? I don't mean to inundate you with this information, but the list is rather extensive and impressive. There are websites that have this information, that are included in this chapter. It is ironic that this is such a well-kept secret. It's public information, but it feels classified.

So what am I proposing by bringing this information to the forefront? What I am proposing is that this information be taught, not only to African Americans, but to all. This should be part of a National Educational Initiative. Instead of NCLB we'll have NEI, from preschool to High School. Just as sure as they are teaching our children that Christopher Columbus discovered America, teach them that it was an African American or a Black man who invented the stethoscope back in Ancient Egypt. Teach them that the air conditioning unit was invented by an African American, teach them that the light bulb, refrigerator, lawn mower, elevator, Blood plasma, almanac, guitar, gas mask, golf tee, horse shoe, mail box, peanut butter, spark plugs, traffic light, typewriter, street sweeper, railway system, rotary engine, fire extinguisher, lock, torpedo discharger, paints, lotions and soaps, automatic fishing reel, shoes, guided missile, airship, fountain pen, sugar refinement, cellular phone, e-mail, urinalysis machine, hydraulic shock absorber, helicopter, fire escape ladder, electric cutoff switch, telephone system, auto airbrake, established blood banks all over the world, and the first open heart surgery, all were invented by African Americans, Negroes, Colored's, whatever you want to call us, except *niggas*. That's just a shortlist. I know you white people are saying that is a bunch of bullshit! *Niggas* ain't did all that! Ain't no way, they could have done all that! Hell, they were still our slaves. Must have been those god-damn Abolitionists that helped them. Damn *nigga lovers*! I guess you're wondering how could I know that those would be the kinds of things

239

you might be saying. Ain't no difference from the way you thought about us back then, than the same way the Executives at Texaco were talking about us amongst themselves in those meetings that were caught on tape. I guess you are dying to see this alleged information, so I think I will insert the website version right here so you can get a taste right now. I must warn you, this information is so shocking, it will probably make you question your self worth to society, especially when you realize that it was us *niggas,* who built this country called America, the Country that all of your ancestors flocked to. The Country you love so deeply. Hope you don't run back to your homeland now that you know the truth and the truth is about to be taught as a National Education Initiative. Take a good look baby! **Black Inventors...Extraordinary Inventions**.

Black Inventors...Extraordinary Inventions!

African Americans have made extraordinary contributions throughout history. A key piece of LittleAfrica.com's mission is to highlight some of those contributions and encourage our community to boldly go after those things that represent a symbol of hope for future generations. These inventors took advantage of their God-given talents to create products that simplified the lives of people all over the world.

Many of you possess similar talent...

It is time for us to leverage that talent, energy, and creativity to make a difference...

Invention	Inventor	Invention	Inventor
Biscuit Cutter	A.P. Ashbourne	**Super Soaker**	Lonnie Johnson
Folding Bed	L.C. Bailey	**Bicycle Frame**	Issac R. Johnson

Item	Inventor	Item	Inventor
Coin Changer	James A. Bauer	Space Shuttle Retrieval Arm	Wm. Harwell
Rotary Engine	Andrew J. Beard	Printing Press	W.A. Lavallette
Car Couple	Andrew J. Beard	Envelope Seal	F.W. Leslie
Letter Box	G.E. Becket	Laser Fuels	Lester Lee
Stainless Steel Pads	Alfred Benjamin	Pressure Cooker	Maurice W. Lee
Torpedo Discharger	H. Bradberry	Window Cleaner	A.L. Lewis
Disposable Syringe	Phil Brooks	Pencil Sharpener	John L. Love
Home Security System	Marie Brown	Fire Extinguisher	Tom J. Marshal
Corn Planter	Henry Blair	Lock	W.A. Martin
Cotton Planter	Henry Blair	Shoe Lasting Machine	Jan Matzeliger
Ironing Board	Sarah Boone	Lubricators	Elijah McCoy
Horse Bridle Bit	L.F.Brown	Rocket Catapult	Hugh MacDonald
Horse shoe	Oscar E. Brown	Elevator	Alexander Miles
Pacemaker	Otis Boykin	Gas Mask	Garrett Morgan
Guide Missile	Otis Boykin	Traffic Signal	Garrett Morgan
Lawn Mower	John A. Burr	Hair Brush	Lyda Newman
Typewriter	Burridge & Marshman	Heating Furnace	Alice H. Paker
Train Alarm	R.A. Butler	Airship	J.F.Pickering
Radiation Detector	Geo. Carruthers	Folding Chair	Purdgy/Sadgwar
Peanut Butter	George W. Carver	Hand Stamp	W.B. Purvis
Paints & Satins	George W. Carver	Fountain Pen	W.B. Purvis
Lotion & Soaps	George W. Carver	Dust Pan	L.P.Ray
Automatic Fishing Reel	George Cook	Insect Destroyer Gun	A.C. Richardson
Ice cream Mold	A.L. Cralle	Baby Buggy	W.H. Richardson
Blood Plasma	Dr. Charles Drew	Sugar Refinement	N. Rillieux
Horse Riding Saddle	Wm. D. Davis	Clothes Dryer	G.T. Sampson
Shoe	W.A. Detiz	Celluar Phone	Henry Sampson
Player Piano	Joseph Dickinson	Pressing Comb	Walter Sammons

Arm for Recording Player	Joseph Dickinson	Curtain Rod	S.R. Scottron
Doorstop	O. Dorsey	Lawn Sprinkler	J.W. Smith
Doorknob	O. Dorsey	Automatic Gearshift	R.B. Spikes
Photo Print Wash	Clatonia J. Dorticus	Urinalysis Machine	Dewey Sanderson
Photo Embossing Machine	Clatonia J. Dorticus	Hydraulic Shock Absorber	Ralph Sanderson
Postal Letter Box	P.B. Dowing	Refrigerator	J. Standard
Toilet	T. Elkins	Mop	T.W. Stewart
Furniture Caster	David A. Fisher	Stairclimbing Wheelchair	Rufus J. Weaver
Guitar	Robert Flemming ,Jr	Helicopter	Paul E. Williams
Golf Tee	George F. Grant	Fire Escape Ladder	J.B. Winters
Motor	J. Gregory	Telephone Transmitter	Granville T. Woods
Lantern	Micheal Harney	Electric Cutoff Switch	Granville T. Woods
Thermo Hair Curlers	Soloman Harper	Relay Instrument	Granville T. Woods
Gas Burner	B.F. Jackson	Telephone System	Granville T. Woods
Kitchen Table	H.A. Jackson	Galvanic Battery	Granville T. Woods
Video Commander	Joseph N. Jackson	Electric Railway System	Granville T. Woods
Remote Controllers	Joseph N. Jackson	Roller Coaster	Granville T. Woods
Sani-Phone	Jerry Johnson	Auto Air Brake	Granville T. Woods

What else do you want to know? Pretty incredible for some former slaves, considering you did everything to destroy us. Almost just as bad as genocide in Dafur. Personally, I would like to know where would you be without these inventions. I would like to know where your tired, your hungry and poor, would have gone if it wasn't for '*our inventions*' that facilitated the American Industrial Revolution?

242

Answer, you would still be where you originally came from. You would still be tired, poor, oppressed, hungry, naked, and hopeless. So I say to my *House Negro*, stop tap dancing and be proud of who you are and where you came from. We come from far more substance than any of them. Only thing they beat us in was killing and stealing. Be proud knowing, it was our inventions, our labor, our fortitude that built this country. I know they treat us like dirt, no, really like shit, but teach your children this information so they can grow up knowing. I graduated from a University and I never knew any of this. Why? I really don't know why, but I do know that we can no longer afford for this not be taught to our children as the real history in America. I'm not talking this being taught as some separate Black History Class, which you know no white person will attend. I'm talking about this being taught at every level of education. We shouldn't stop advocating for something like this. It's non confrontational, it's true, and unlike that whole thing about Christopher Columbus discovering America, nothing personal, but that's so far from the truth, yet we even have a holiday for it. How long can this Country continue to hide behind its white lies? I know they are going to be afraid of this, but what is there to fear? We invented all this, during a time when we couldn't even vote, and had no rights. Leaves me to wonder how many inventions were stolen from us. But we aren't here and the NEI isn't here to discuss the grave injustices we suffered at the hands of the white slave masters of this Country. We are here to discuss the incorporation of our contributions, which aided this society in being able to offer the world to bring their tired, their hungry and their poor over here for a better life and opportunity. All I'm saying is that if you look at these inventions, you have to admit that there is a direct correlation to the Industrial Revolution, which was the beginning of America becoming America the beautiful for some, even though liberty and justice is supposed to be for all. Well, this will be our liberty and justice, the incorporation of African American inventions into America's History. As I stated in the previous chapter, their ain't no Race who can say they have made the contributions to society that we have made. None! No not one, not anybody! So again, be proud *House Negro*, because by acting like a *house- nigga* you bring shame and disgrace to our people. I truly hope this will enlighten you and aid in your development and awareness of who you are and how important it is for you to be a proud Black individual. I hope you read or go through this extensive list of Black Inventions, and it inspires you as it has given me hope for our future and hope for this nation to finally stand up to the true meaning of its creed. Yeah right! I can see it and hear it now, well if they invented all these things etc., etc., then why are they not the head of these corporations, or economically in the forefront of all of us? My response to that is relatively simple. If you want to get into the ill-effects of slavery, if you want to take a real good look at how damaging and destructive racial discrimination is, if you want to look at the cruelty and injustices that have been placed upon my people and the injustices that continue to plague my people, simply because of the color of their skin, then and only then will you find out why we are where we are. Now, if you want to look at that, we can, however, I am sure you don't really want to do that, because you would have to look at all the cruel realities of your ancestors of not so long ago. So the choice is yours. We can go there, or we can just leave it as is. You can challenge the validity of the Black contribution to this society or continue to hide your exploits of the Black Man in America and Africa. Are you really that afraid of us? I know, we should want to kill all of you for the brutality you have inflicted upon us from enslaving us, the raping of our women, the killing of our children and the destruction of our families, but then we would have to kill the whole world because you all were conspirators. So lets call a truce, a peace treaty. Lets start off with the introduction of Black Inventions in American society as part of the National Educational Initiative. OK! C'mon, don't be scared, it's just education. After all, isn't education the key to success? And when you consider the shape our schools are in today, maybe something like this could be the beginning of a new day for all of us. Actually, I'm betting on it. This could reach far and wide, especially if white people don't take all of their children out of public schools and make sure they don't teach their children any of this knowledge in private schools. This could actually reach across the seas to all nations. After all, the whole world is here in America anyway. Now I know that there are those who believe in the New World Order and are going to fight this and have fits about this, but guess what, this is the

New World Order! That's right, an attempt to correct the injustices and atrocities inflicted upon an entire race. Not monetarily, like the call for reparations, but through education. I ask, I implore you to join me in this effort, and realize that when we succeed, the world succeeds, as evidenced in our inventions that fueled the Industrial Revolution and the ability for your fore-parents to have the opportunity to come to America, from out of the despair and poverty that encompassed them. Conversely, you need to realize that when we fail so does everyone else. Look at where we are today as a nation. Look at gas prices. This Country is failing. Look at our position in the world globally. We owe China two hundred and two billion dollars, and it's rising every day. It's ridiculous. Yes, the rich are still getting richer and the poor poorer, and if we don't correct this two-class society trend, we will be on the verge of a communistic state. I guess since we owe China so much money that would work out just fine. We must be ever so careful, especially when you consider the necessities of security since 9/11, that we protect our democracy.

Look at the Black male unemployment rate, 58%, not to mention underemployment. When the Black male was being employed through Affirmative Action, this Country was on the cusp of greatness. I truly do believe that there is this direct correlation between the success of this Country and the success of the African American. And even if you don't think so, China is sure doing some serious business in Africa and the development of oil, and is going to change our position as number one. Look at GM, scared to death. Please, wake up before it's too late. Toyota is now number one in the automotive industry. I know the thought of a Black President scares the hell out of all of you, but you might want to think about it. By the way, I am not talking about Obama! It might be our only hope! As long as we are barred from the possibilities and opportunities that America has to offer, then the Pledge of Allegiance is nothing more than a hypocritical oath. This Country will not be able to survive much longer living a lie. Conversely, however, this Country could become the greatest Empire to ever grace the face of the Earth.

I leave you with this. It's time to represent, no more excuses. We must unite in order to survive. It's like a company that needs to merge in order to strengthen its competitive edge. We must find a way to work together again. Everyone comes here legally or illegally to find a better life. Gives you an idea of what's really happening across the globe. They come here for a better life and opportunity. They use us, take our money and send it back home. I'm not saying it's wrong to send money back home to help out the people in your country, but I question the loyalty to this Country. The African American's history with this Country is inseparable, yet slavery has prohibited us from working together. We must legitimately attempt to rectify this breach so we can maintain our leadership role and be an example for the whole world to emulate. Never in the history of man has there ever been such a union between the once oppressed and the oppressor, or the once slave and the once slave master. Can we rise to represent the epitome of a society, or will we fall like the diaries of Communism suggest of Capitalism? I pray not, I hope not! Not only for myself, but for our children's sake. Can we not unite to save our children? Will we not unite if unification means preserving our role in the world? Britain once ruled many colonies, was the leading power in the world. Will we ultimately become a secondary power? I pray not, I hope not! I remember all too well how Texaco fell to Chevron. First there was a partnership where Texaco was the majority stakeholder, and didn't have any reservations about making the employees of Chevron aware of that. Like they say, payback is a you know what! And when Chevron took over Texaco, boy oh boy was it payback time. Poetic justice? There is a saying that goes, 'be careful how you treat people on your way up because those are the same ones you will see on the way coming down'. I think that is one of the great fears that keeps the white race from doing the right thing. They have done so much, to so many, for so long, that they are afraid they may reap what they have sown. I guess I would be concerned about our empowerment also if I was white. I would fear reaping all that I have sown on the Black people in America. Imagine reaping the cruelty of slavery, and all the other injustices throughout the ages placed upon our Race. But at this point, all retaliation would accomplish is the destruction of us both. I pray not, I hope not, for the sakes of Blacks and American whites in the future. Let this be a reason for us to move forward to the future. No more *House Negro*es to sell us out, or to sell us ever again. Our dignity is no longer for sale. "Blacks to the Future" a new future, a future of promise, hope and success for all. It really is possible. 'Dream the impossible dream'. Educate yourselves and your children to the true history of the African American in America. I recently shared this information with some young Black males in the 'Hood', my new residency. You should have seen the amazement and the pride on their faces as they scanned through the information of Black Inventors and Inventions. That's when I knew without a doubt, that this information could have a great impact upon society. As their friends passed by, they shared the information with them. It was like, "Yo, check this shit out!" Did you know that a Black man created this and a Black man created that? Did you know that a Black man invented the Space Shuttle retrieval arm? And you wonder why they don't want to go to school to continue learning all this other bullshit you keep forcing them to eat. I saw pride and dignity reemerge. A revalidation of being proud to be Black. It was incredible! It was exciting to see! It was hope! It was life! It was birth! It was truth! I wonder how white people will respond to such information? Maybe they will feel the exact opposite when they come to realize that if it was not for our Race their life would be garbage. Man, that's a bitter pill to swallow. No wonder they have to oppress our contributions. This is really sad and disheartening, but Black Inventions is not for the purpose of bringing you down to your true reality, but for the sole purpose of bringing the truth to light. So I bring you now to the Patent Process. Hell, if you think Black Inventors Extraordinary Inventions was something, this document has the inventor, the date and the patent number to go with it, for all of you skeptics and non- believers. I bet you could probably find some asinine *House Negro* to say this document is fraudulent and why this colored boy want to make trouble, talking this nonsense. We jus fine massa, ain't we! I know you white people are probably gonna have a heart-attack when you read this, but just remember, it was a Black man who performed the first successful open heart surgery. I give you, The Patent Process, the New Educational Initiative.

Peace, I'm out, Mission Accomplished!

APPENDIX

BLACK INVENTORS AND INVENTIONS

"Only when lions have historians will hunters cease being heroes." ~ African Proverb

Inventor Links:
Black Inventors
the african american invention express

Product	Inventor	Date
air conditioning unit	Frederick M. Jones	July 12, 1949
almanac	Benjamin Banneker	Approx 1791
auto cut-off switch	Granville T. Woods	January 1, 1839
auto fishing devise	G. Cook	May 30, 1899
automatic gear shift	Richard Spikes	February 28, 1932
baby buggy	W.H. Richardson	June 18, 1899
bicycle frame	L.R. Johnson	October 10, 1899
biscuit cutter	A.P. Ashbourne	November 30, 1875
blood plasma bag	Charles Drew	Approx. 1945
cellular phone	Henry T. Sampson	July 6, 1971
chamber commode	T. Elkins	January 3, 1897
clothes dryer	G. T. Sampson	June 6, 1862
curtain rod	S. R. Scratton	November 30, 1889
curtain rod support	William S. Grant	August 4, 1896
door knob	O. Dorsey	December 10, 1878
door stop	O. Dorsey	December 10, 1878
dust pan	Lawrence P. Ray	August 3, 1897
egg beater	Willie Johnson	February 5, 1884
electric lampbulb	Lewis Latimer	March 21, 1882
elevator	Alexander Miles	October 11, 1867
eye protector	P. Johnson	November 2, 1880
fire escape ladder	J. W. Winters	May 7, 1878
fire extinguisher	T. Marshall	October 26, 1872
folding bed	L. C. Bailey	July 18, 1899
folding chair	Brody & Surgwar	June 11, 1889
fountain pen	W. B. Purvis	January 7, 1890
furniture caster	O. A. Fisher	1878
gas mask	Garrett Morgan	October 13, 1914
golf tee	T. Grant	December 12, 1899
guitar	Robert F. Flemming, Jr.	March 3, 1886
hair brush	Lydia O. Newman	November 15, 18--
hand stamp	Walter B. Purvis	February 27 1883
horse shoe	J. Ricks	March 30, 1885
ice cream scooper	A. L. Cralle	February 2, 1897
improv. sugar making	Norbet Rillieux	December 10, 1846
insect-destroyer gun	A. C. Richard	February 28, 1899
ironing board	Sarah Boone	December 30, 1887
key chain	F. J. Loudin	January 9, 1894
lantern	Michael C. Harvey	August 19, 1884
lawn mower	L. A. Burr	May 19, 1889
lawn sprinkler	J. W. Smith	May 4, 1897
lemon squeezer	J. Thomas White	December 8, 1893
lock	W. A. Martin	July 23, 18--
lubricating cup	Ellijah McCoy	November 15, 1895
lunch pail	James Robinson	1887
mail box	Paul L. Downing	October 27, 1891
mop	Thomas W. Stewart	June 11, 1893
motor	Frederick M. Jones	June 27, 1939
peanut butter	George Washington Carver	1896

253

Black Inventors and Inventions

The following African Americans are responsible for either inventing, or improving on the invention of, a wide variety of items. From Dr. Charles Drew to Garrett A. Morgan, the inventions of African Americans have played a large role in AMERICAN history.

Andrew Beard - Automatic Car Coupling Device (1897)

Henry Blair
- Mechanical Seed Planter (1834)
- Mechanical Corn Harvester (1836)

C. B. Brooks - Street Sweeper (1896)

Mark Dean - Microcomputer system with bus control means for peripheral processing devices (1984)

Dr. Charles Drew - Established Blood Banks all over the world (1940)

W. Johnson - Egg Beater (1884)

Frederick Jones
- Refrigeration for transport trucks (1938)
- Refrigeration for railroad cars (1945)

J. L. Love - Pencil Sharpener (1897)

Elijah McCoy - Automatic Lubrication System for railroads and heavy machinery (1892)

Jan Matzeliger - Automatic Shoe Making Machine that revolutionized the making of shoes (1883)

Alexander Miles - Elevator (1888)

Garrett A. Morgan
- Gas Mask that saved many lives during WWI (1914)
- Automatic Traffic Signal (1923)

Norbett Rillieux - Sugar Refining System that revolutionized the making of sugar (1846)

W. H. Sammons - Hot Comb (1920)

Lewis Temple - Toggle Harpoon (1848)

Dr. Daniel Hale Williams - First Open Heart Surgery (1893)

Black Inventors...Extraordinary Inventions!

African Americans have made extraordinary contributions throughout history. A key piece of LittleAfrica.com's mission is to highlight some of those contributions and encourage our community to boldly go after those things that represent a symbol of hope for future generations. These inventors took advantage of their God-given talents to create products that simplified the lives of people all over the world.

Many of you possess similar talent...

It is time for us to leverage that talent, energy, and creativity to make a difference...

Invention	Inventor	Invention	Inventor
Biscuit Cutter	A.P. Ashbourne	Super Soaker	Lonnie Johnson
Folding Bed	L.C. Bailey	Bicycle Frame	Issac R. Johnson
Coin Changer	James A. Bauer	Space Shuttle Retrieval Arm	Wm. Harwell
Rotary Engine	Andrew J. Beard	Printing Press	W.A. Lavallette
Car Couple	Andrew J. Beard	Envelope Seal	F.W. Leslie
Letter Box	G.E. Becket	Laser Fuels	Lester Lee
Stainless Steel Pads	Alfred Benjamin	Pressure Cooker	Maurice W. Lee
Torpedo Discharger	H. Bradberry	Window Cleaner	A.L. Lewis
Disposable Syringe	Phil Brooks	Pencil Sharpener	John L. Love
Home Security System	Marie Brown	Fire Extinguisher	Tom J. Marshal
Corn Planter	Henry Blair	Lock	W.A. Martin
Cotton Planter	Henry Blair	Shoe Lasting Machine	Jan Matzeliger
Ironing Board	Sarah Boone	Lubricators	Elijah McCoy
Horse Bridle Bit	L.F.Brown	Rocket Catapult	Hugh MacDonald

Horse shoe	Oscar E. Brown	Elevator	Alexander Miles
Pacemaker	Otis Boykin	Gas Mask	Garrett Morgan
Guide Missile	Otis Boykin	Traffic Signal	Garrett Morgan
Lawn Mower	John A. Burr	Hair Brush	Lyda Newman
Typewriter	Burridge & Marshman	Heating Furnace	Alice H. Paker
Train Alarm	R.A. Butler	Airship	J.F.Pickering
Radiation Detector	Geo. Carruthers	Folding Chair	Purdgy/Sadgwar
Peanut Butter	George W. Carver	Hand Stamp	W.B. Purvis
Paints & Satins	George W. Carver	Fountain Pen	W.B. Purvis
Lotion & Soaps	George W. Carver	Dust Pan	L.P.Ray
Automatic Fishing Reel	George Cook	Insect Destroyer Gun	A.C. Richardson
Ice cream Mold	A.L. Cralle	Baby Buggy	W.H. Richardson
Blood Plasma	Dr. Charles Drew	Sugar Refinement	N. Rillieux
Horse Riding Saddle	Wm. D. Davis	Clothes Dryer	G.T. Sampson
Shoe	W.A. Detiz	Celluar Phone	Henry Sampson
Player Piano	Joseph Dickinson	Pressing Comb	Walter Sammons
Arm for Recording Player	Joseph Dickinson	Curtain Rod	S.R. Scottron
Doorstop	O. Dorsey	Lawn Sprinkler	J.W. Smith
Doorknob	O. Dorsey	Automatic Gearshift	R.B. Spikes
Photo Print Wash	Clatonia J. Dorticus	Urinalysis Machine	Dewey Sanderson
Photo Embossing Machine	Clatonia J. Dorticus	Hydraulic Shock Absorber	Ralph Sanderson
Postal Letter Box	P.B. Dowing	Refrigerator	J. Standard
Toilet	T. Elkins	Mop	T.W. Stewart
Furniture Caster	David A. Fisher	Stairclimbing Wheelchair	Rufus J. Weaver
Guitar	Robert Flemming ,Jr	Helicopter	Paul E. Williams
Golf Tee	George F. Grant	Fire Escape Ladder	J.B. Winters

Motor	J. Gregory	**Telephone Transmitter**	Granville T. Woods
Lantern	Micheal Harney	**Electric Cutoff Switch**	Granville T. Woods
Thermo Hair Curlers	Soloman Harper	**Relay Instrument**	Granville T. Woods
Gas Burner	B.F. Jackson	**Telephone System**	Granville T. Woods
Kitchen Table	H.A. Jackson	**Galvanic Battery**	Granville T. Woods
Video Commander	Joseph N. Jackson	**Electric Railway System**	Granville T. Woods
Remote Controllers	Joseph N. Jackson	**Roller Coaster**	Granville T. Woods
Sani-Phone	Jerry Johnson	**Auto Air Brake**	Granville T. Woods

Granville Woods
- Multiplex Telegraph system, allowing messages to be sent/received from moving trains (1887)
- Railway Air Brakes that provided the first safe method of stopping trains (1903)
- Steam-boiler/radiator (1884)
- Third Rail [subway] (1893)

J. T. White - Lemon Squeezer (1896)

*For more inforamation, visit the **About.com Black Inventors Page**.*

Return to AA History Home | Return to Rites of Passage Home

THE PATENT PROCESS

The first patent act in the United States was signed by George Washington, in 1790, with only three patents being granted during the first year. It is anticipated that four million patents will have been issued by 1980. The first patent known to have been granted to a Black man was issued to Henry Blair, of Maryland, for a cornplanting machine.

A patent lasts 17 years. Fundamentals of the patent system are, in general, that any person who has invented any new, useful, novel process; new machine, manufacturing process, or composition of matter; and also certain varieties of plants, or improvements thereto, . . . may obtain a patent!

The first condition requires that the invention must not have been previously patented or described in any printed publication in any country, or in public use, or c sale in *this* country. The second condition stipulates that the invention be operative for a useful purpose. In early days it was necessary to have constructed a "working" model. The third condition recites the degree of ingenuity or cleverness needed to warrant a patent: It must be "unobvious" to the "skilled" person in the art.

Patents are grouped under one or another of some 340 headings. These in turn are broken down into 80,000 subject groups. (Recent new approaches and computerized restructuring of procedures have slightly changed this classification.) There are three broad, "generic" divisions of patents: mechanical, design, and reissue. However, 90 per cent of patents granted come under the heading of "mechanical," and have a life of 17 years. Design patents refer generally to novel and ingenious appearances . . . such as furniture, lampshades, fabric patterns, shoe styles, and the decorations on dishes. Such design patents may be obtained for terms of 3, 7, or 14 years.

Inventor	Invention	Date	Patent
Brooks, C. B.	Punch	Oct. 31, 1893	507,672
Brooks, C. B.	Street Sweepers	Mar. 17, 1896	556,711
Brooks, C. B.	Street Sweepers	May 12, 1896	560,154
Brooks, Hallstead and Page	Street Sweepers	Apr. 21, 1896	558,719
Brown, Henry	Receptacle for Storing and Preserving Papers	Nov. 2, 1886	352,036
Brown, L. F.	Bridle Bit	Oct 25, 1892	484,994
Brown, O. E.	Horseshoe	Aug. 23, 1892	481,271
Brown & Latimer	Water Closets for Railway Cars	Feb. 10, 1874	147,363
Burr, J. A.	Lawn Mower	May 9, 1899	624,749
Burr, W. F.	Switching Device for Railways	Oct. 31, 1899	636,197
Burwell, W.	Boot or Shoe	Nov. 28, 1899	638,143
Butler, R. A.	Train Alarm	June 15, 1897	584,540
Butts, J. W.	Luggage Carrier	Oct. 10, 1899	634,611
Byrd, T. J.	Improvement in Holders for Reins for Horses	Feb. 6, 1872	123,328
Byrd, T. J.	Apparatus for Detaching Horses from Carriages	Mar. 19, 1872	124,790
Byrd, T. J.	Improvement in Neck Yokes for Wagons	Apr. 30, 1872	126,181
Byrd, T. J.	Improvement in Car Couplings	Dec. 1, 1874	157,370
Campbell, W. S.	Self-Setting Animal Trap	Aug. 30, 1881	246,369
Cargill, B. F.	Invalid Cot	July 25, 1899	629,658
Carrington, T. A.	Range	July 25, 1876	180,323
Carter, W. C.	Umbrella Stand	Aug. 4, 1885	323,397
Certain, J. M.	Parcel Carrier for Bicycles	Dec. 26, 1899	639,708
Cherry, M. A.	Velocipede	May 8, 1888	382,351
Cherry, M. A.	Street Car Fender	Jan. 1, 1895	531,908
Church, T. S.	Carpet Beating Machine	July 29, 1884	302,237
Clare, O. B.	Trestle	Oct. 9, 1888	390,753
Coates, R.	Overboot for Horses	Apr. 19, 1892	473,295
Cook, G.	Automatic Fishing Device	May 30, 1899	625,829
Coolidge, J. S.	Harness Attachment	Nov. 13, 1888	392,908
Cooper, A. R.	Shoemaker's Jack	Aug. 22, 1899	631,519
Cooper, J.	Shutter and Fastening	May 1, 1883	276,563
Cooper, J.	Elevator Device	Apr. 2, 1895	536,605
Cooper, J.	Elevator Device	Spe. 21, 1897	590,257

Inventor	Invention	Date	Patent
Cornwell, P. W.	Draft Regulator	Oct. 2, 1888	390,284
Cornwell, P. W.	Draft Regulator	Feb. 7, 1893	491,082
Cralle, A. L.	Ice-Cream Mold	Feb. 2, 1897	576,395
Creamer, H.	Steam Feed Water Trap	Mar. 17, 1895	313,854
Creamer, H.	Steam Trap Feeder	Dec. 11, 1888	394,463
(Creamer also patented five steam traps between 1887 and 1893)			
Cosgrove, W. F.	Automatic Stop Plug for Gas Oil Pipes	Mar. 17, 1885	313,993
Darkins, J. T.	Ventilation Aid	Feb 19, 1895	534,322
Davis, I. D.	Tonic	Nov. 2, 1886	351,829
Davis, W. D.	Riding Saddles	Oct. 6, 1896	568,939
Davis, W. R., Jr.	Library Table	Sep. 24, 1878	208,378
Deitz, W. A.	Shoe	Apr. 30, 1867	64,205
Dickinson, J. H.	Pianola	Detroit, Mich. 1899	
Dorsey, O.	Door-Holding Device	Dec. 10, 1878	210,764
Dorticus, C. J.	Device/Applying Coloring/sides of Shoe soles	Mar 19, 1895	535,820
Dorticus, C. J.	Machine for Embossing Photo	Apr. 16, 1895	537,442
Dorticus, C. J.	Photographic Print Wash	Apr. 23, 1895	537,968
Dorticus, C. J.	Hose Leak Stop	July 18, 1899	629,315
Downing, P. B.	Electric Switch for Railroad	June 17, 1890	430,118
Downing, P. B.	Letter Box	Oct. 27, 1891	462,093
Downing, P. B.	Street Letter Box	Oct. 27, 1891	462,096
Dunnington, J. H.	Horse Detachers	Mar. 16, 1897	578,979
Edmonds, T. H.	Separating Screens	July 20, 1897	586,724
Elkins, T.	Dining/Ironing Table/Quilting Frame Combined	Feb. 22, 1870	100,020
Elkins, T.	Chamber Commode	Jan 9, 1872	122,518
Elkins, T.	Refrigerating Apparatus	Nov. 4, 1879	221,222
Evans, J. H.	Convertible Settees	Oct. 5, 1897	591,095
Faulkner, H.	Ventilated Shoe	Apr. 29, 1890	426,495
Ferrell, F. J.	Steam Trap	Feb. 11, 1890	420,993
Ferrell, F. J.	Apparatus for Melting Snow	May 27, 1890	428,670
(Ferrell also patented eight valves between 1890 and 1893.)			

260

Inventor	Invention	Date	Patent
Fisher, D. A.	Joiner's Clamp	Apr. 20, 1875	162,281
Fisher, D. A.	Furniture Castor	Mar. 14, 1876	174,794
Flemming, R. F., Jr.	Guitar	Mar. 3, 1886	338,727
Forten, J.	Sail Control	Mass. Newspaper 1850	
Goode, Sarah E.	Folding Cabinet Bed	July 14, 1885	322,177
Grant, G. F.	Golf Tee	Dec. 12, 1899	638,920
Grant, W. S.	Curtain Rod Support	Aug. 4, 1896	565,075
Gray, R. H.	Baling Press	Aug. 28, 1894	525,203
Gray, R. H.	Cistern Cleaners	Apr. 9, 1895	537,151
Gregory, J.	Motor	Apr. 26, 1887	361,937
Grenon, H.	Razor Stropping Device	Feb. 18, 1896	554,867
Griffin, F. W.	Pool Table Attachment	June 13, 1899	626,902
Gunn, S. W.	Boot or Shoe	Jan. 16, 1900	641,642
Haines, J. H.	Portable Basin	Sep. 28, 1897	590,833
Hammonds, J. F.	Apparatus for Holding Yarn Skeins	Dec. 15, 1986	572,985
Harding, F. H.	Extension Banquet Table	Nov. 22, 1898	614,468
Hawkins, J.	Gridiron	Mar. 26, 1845	3,973
Hawkins, R.	Harness Attachment	Oct. 4, 1887	370,943
Headen, M.	Foot Power Hammer	Oct. 5, 1886	350,363
Hearness, R.	Sealing Attachment for Bottles	Feb. 15, 1898	598,929
Hearness, R.	Detachable Car Fender	July 4, 1899	628,003
Hilyer, A. F.	Water Evaporator Attach./Hot Air Registers	Aug. 26, 1890	435,095
Hilyer, A. F.	Registers	Oct. 14, 1890	438,159
Holmes, E. H.	Gage	Nov. 12, 1895	549,513
Hunter, J. H.	Portable Weighing Scales	Nov 3, 1896	570,553
Hyde, R. N.	Composition for Cleaning/Preserving Carpets	Nov. 6, 1888	392,205
Jackson, B. F.	Heating Apparatus	Mar. 1, 1898	599,985
Jackson, B. F.	Matrix Drying Apparatus	May 10, 1898	603,879
Jackson, B. F.	Gas Burner	Apr. 4, 1899	622,482
Jackson, H. A.	Kitchen Table	Oct 6, 1896	596,135
Jackson, W. H.	Railway Switch	Mar. 9, 1897	578,641

Inventor	Invention	Date	Patent
Jackson, W. H.	Railway Switch	Mar. 16, 1897	593,665
Jackson, W. H.	Automatic Locking Switch	Aug. 23, 1898	609,436
Johnson, D.	Rotary Dining Table	Jan. 15, 1888	396,089
Johnson, D.	Lawn Mower Attachment	Sep. 10, 1889	410,836
Johnson, D.	Grass Receivers for Lawn Mowers	June 10, 1890	429,629
Johnson, I. R.	Bicycle Frame	Oct. 10, 1899	634,823
Johnson, P.	Swinging Chairs	Nov. 15, 1881	249,530
Johnson, P.	Eye Protector	Nov. 2, 1880	234,039
Johnson, W.	Velocipede	June 20, 1899	627,335
Johnson, W. A.	Paint Vehicle	Dec. 4, 1888	393,763
Johnson, W. H.	Overcoming Dead Centers	Feb. 4, 1896	554,223
Johnson, W. H.	Overcoming Dead Centers	Oct. 11, 1898	612,345
Johnson, W.	Egg Beater	Feb. 5, 1884	292,821
Jones, F. M.	Ticket Dispensing Machine	June 27, 1939	2,163,754
Jones, F. M.	Air Conditioning Unit	July 12, 1949	2,475,841
Jones, F. M.	Method for Air Conditioning	Dec. 7, 1954	2,696,086
Jones, F. M.	Method for Preserving Perishables	Feb. 12, 1957	2,780,923
Jones, F. M.	Two-Cycle Gasoline Engine	Nov. 28, 1950	2,523,273
Jones, F. M.	Two-Cycle Gas Engine	May 29, 1945	2,376,968
Jones, F. M.	Starter Generator	July 12, 1949	2,475,842
Jones, F. M.	Starter Generator for Cooling Gas Engines		2,475,843
Jones, F. M.	Two-Cycle Gas Engine	Mar. 11, 1947	2,417,253
Jones, F. M.	Means/Thermostatically Operating Gas Engines	July 26, 1949	2,477,377
Jones, F. M.	Rotary Compressor	Apr. 18, 1950	2,504,841
Jones, F. M.	System/Controlling Refrigeration Units	May 23, 1950	2,509,099
Jones, F. M.	Heating/Cooling Atmosphere within Enclosure	Oct 24, 1950	2,526,874
Jones, F. M.	Prefabricated Refrigerator Construction	Dec. 26, 1950	2,535,682
Jones, F. M.	Refrigeration Control Device	Jan. 8, 1952	2,581,956
Jones, F. M.	Methods/Means of Defrosting a Cold Diffuser	Jan. 19, 1954	2,666,298
Jones, F. M.	Control Device for Internal Combustion Engine	Sep. 2, 1958	2,850,001
Jones, F. M.	Thermostat and Temperature Control System	Feb. 23, 1960	2,926,005
Jones, F. M.	Removable Cooling Units for Compartments		2,336,735
Jones, F. M.	Means for Automatically Stopping & Starting Gas Engines ("J. A. Numero et al")	Dec. 21, 1943	2,337,164

Inventor	Invention	Date	Patent
Jones, F. M.	Design for Air Conditioning Unit	July 4, 1950	159,209
Jones, F. M.	Design for Air Conditioning Unit	Apr. 28, 1942	132,182
Jones & Long	Caps for Bottles	Sep. 13, 1898	610,715
Joyce, J. A.	Ore Bucket	Apr. 26, 1898	603,143
Latimer & Brown	Water Closets for Railway Cars	Feb. 10, 1874	147,363
Latimer, L. H.	Manufacturing Carbons	June 17, 1882	252,386
Latimer, L. H.	Apparatus for Cooling and Disinfecting	Jan. 12, 1886	334,078
Latimer, L. H.	Locking Racks for Coats, Hats, and Umbrellas	Mar. 24, 1896	557,076
Latimer & Nichols	Electric Lamp	Sep. 13, 1881	247,097
Latimer & Tregoning	Globe Support for Electric Lamps	Mar. 21, 1882	255,212
Lavalette, W. A.	Printing Press	Sep. 17, 1878	208,208
Lee, H	Animal Trap	Feb. 12, 1867	61,941
Lee, J.	Kneading Machine	Aug. 7, 1894	524,042
Lee, J.	Break Crumbing Machine	June 4, 1895	540,553
Leslie, F. W.	Envelope Seal	Sep. 21, 1897	590,325
Lewis, A. L.	Window Cleaner	Sep. 27, 1892	483,359
Lewis, E. R.	Spring Gun	May 3, 1887	362,096
Linden, H.	Piano Truck	Sep. 8, 1891	459,365
Little, E.	Bridle-Bit	Mar. 7, 1882	254,666
Loudin, F. J.	Sash Fastener	Dec. 12, 1892	510,432
Loudin, F. J.	Key Fastener	Jan. 9, 1894	512,308
Love, J. L.	Plasterers' Hawk	July 9, 1895	542,419
Love, J. L.	Pencil Sharpener	Nov. 23, 1897	594,114
Marshall, T. J.	Fire Extinguisher	May 26, 1872	125,063
Marshall, W.	Grain Binder	May 11, 1886	341,599
Martin, W. A.	Lock	July 23, 1889	407,738
Martin, W. A.	Lock	Dec. 30, 1890	443,945
Matzeliger, J. E.	Mechanism for Distributing Tacks	Nov. 26, 1899	415,726
Matzeliger, J. E.	Nailing Machine	Feb. 25, 1896	421,954
Matzeliger, J. E.	Tack Separating Mechanism	Mar. 25, 1890	423,937
Matzeliger, J. E.	Lasting Machine	Sep. 22, 1891	459,899
McCoy, E. J.	Lubricator	May 27, 1873	139,407

Inventor	Invention	Date	Patent
McCoy, E. J.	Lubricator	Mar. 28, 1882	255,443
McCoy, E. J.	Lubricator	July 18, 1882	261,166
McCoy, E. J.	Lubricator	June 16, 1885	320,379
McCoy, E. J.	Lubricator	Feb. 8, 1887	357,491
McCoy, E. J.	Lubricator	May 29, 1888	383,745
McCoy, E. J.	Lubricator	May 29, 1888	383,746
McCoy, E. J.	Lubricator	Dec. 24, 1899	418,139
McCoy, E. J.	Lubricator	Dec. 29, 1891	465,875
McCoy, E. J.	Lubricator	Apr. 5, 1892	472,066
McCoy, E. J.	Lubricator	Sep. 13, 1898	610,634
McCoy, E. J.	Lubricator	Oct. 4, 1898	611,759
McCoy, E. J.	Oil Cup	Nov. 15, 1898	614,307
McCoy, E. J.	Lubricator	June 27, 1899	627,623
McCoy, E. J.	Lubricator for Steam Engines	July 2, 1872	129,843
McCoy, E. J.	Lubricator for Steam Engines	Aug. 6, 1872	130,305
McCoy, E. J.	Steam Lubricator	Jan. 20, 1874	146,697
McCoy, E. J.	Ironing Table	May 12, 1874	150,876
McCoy, E. J.	Steam Cylinder Lubricator	Feb. 1, 1876	173,032
McCoy, E. J.	Steam Cylinder Lubricator	July 4, 1876	179,585
McCoy, E. J.	Lawn Sprinkler Design	Sep. 26, 1899	631,549
McCoy, E. J.	Steam Dome	June 16, 1885	320,354
McCoy, E. J.	Lubricator Attachment	Apr. 19, 1887	361,435
McCoy, E. J.	Lubricator for Safety Valves	May 24, 1887	363,529
McCoy, E. J.	Drip Cup	Sep. 29, 1891	460,215
McCoy & Hodges	Lubricator	Dec. 24, 1889	418,139
McCree, D.	Portable Fire Escape	Nov. 11, 1890	440,322
Mendenhall, A.	Holder for Driving Reins	Nov. 289, 1899	637,811
Miles, A.	Elevator	Oct. 11, 1887	371,207
Mitchell, C. L.	Phneterisin	Jan. 1, 1884	291,071
Mitchell, J. M.	Check Row Corn Planter	Jan. 16, 1900	641,462
Moody, W. U.	Game Board Design	May 11, 1897	27,046
Morehead, K.	Reel Carrier	Oct. 6, 1896	568,916
Murray, G. W.	Combined Furrow Opener and Stalk-Knocker	Apr. 10, 1894	517,960
Murray, G. W.	Cultivator and Marker	Apr. 10, 1894	517,961

Inventor	Invention	Date	Patent
Murray, G. W.	Planter	June 5, 1894	520,887
Murray, G. W.	Cotton Chopper	June 5, 1894	520,888
Murray, G. W.	Fertilizer Distributor	June 5, 1894	520,889
Murray, G. W.	Planter	June 5, 1894	520,890
Murray, G. W.	Combined Cotton Seed	June 5, 1894	520,891
Murray, G. W.	Planter and Fertilizer Distributor Reaper	June 5, 1894	520,892
Murray, W.	Attachment for Bicycles	Jan. 27, 1891	445,452
Nance, L.	Game Apparatus	De. 1, 1891	464,035
Nash, H. H.	Life Preserving Stool	Oct. 5, 1875	168,519
Newman, L. D.	Brush	Nov. 15, 1898	614,335
Newson, S.	Oil Heater or Cooker	May 22, 1894	520,188
Nichols & Latimer	Electric Lamp	Sep. 13, 1881	247,097
Nickerson, W. J.	Mandolin and Guitar Attachment for Pianos	June 27, 1899	627,739
O'Connor & Turner	Alarm for Boilers	Aug. 25, 1896	566,612
O'Connor & Turner	Steam Gage	Aug. 25, 1896	566,613
O'Connor & Turner	Alarm for Coasts Containing Vessels	Feb. 8, 1898	598,572
Outlaw, J. W.	Horseshoes	Nov. 15, 1898	614,273
Perryman, F. R.	Caterers' Tray Table	Feb. 2, 1892	468,038
Peterson, H.	Attachment for Lawn Mowers	Apr. 30, 1889	402,189
Phelps, W. H.	Apparatus for Washing Vehicles	Mar. 23, 1897	579,242
Pickering, J. F.	Air Ship	Feb. 20, 1900	643,975
Pickett, H.	Scaffold	June 30, 1874	152,511
Pinn, T. B.	File Holder	Aug. 17, 1880	231,355
Polk, A. J.	Bicycle Support	Apr. 14, 1896	558,103
Pugsley, A.	Blind Stop	July 29, 1890	433,306
Purdy & Peters	Design for Spoons	Apr. 23, 1895	24,228
Purdy & Sadgwar	Folding Chair	June 11, 1889	405,117
Purdy, W.	Device for Sharpening Edged Tools	Oct. 27, 1896	570,337
Purdy, W.	Design for Sharpening Edged Tools	Aug. 16, 1898	609,367
Purdy, W.	Device for Sharpening Edged Tools	Aug. 1, 1899	630,106
Purvis, W. B.	Bag Fastener	Apr. 25, 1882	256,856

Inventor	Invention	Date	Patent
Purvis, W. B.	Hand Stamp	Feb. 27, 1883	273,149
Purvis, W. B.	Fountain Pen	Jan. 7, 1890	419,065
Purvis, W. B.	Electric Railway	May 1, 1894	519,291
Purvis, W. B.	Magnetic Car Balancing Device	May 21, 1895	539,542
Purvis, W. B.	Electric Railway Switch	Aug. 17, 1897	588,176

(Purvis also patented ten paper bag machines between 1884 and 1894.)

Inventor	Invention	Date	Patent
Queen, W.	Guard for Companion Ways and Hatches	Aug. 18, 1891	458,131
Ray, E. P.	Chair Supporting Device	Feb. 21, 1899	620,078
Ray, L. P.	Dust Pan	Aug. 3, 1897	587,607
Reed, J. W.	Dough Kneader and Roller	Sep. 23, 1884	305,474
Reynolds, H. H.	Window Ventilator for Railroad Cars	Apr. 3, 1883	275,271
Reynolds, H. H.	Safety Gate for Bridges	Oct. 7, 1890	437,937
Reynolds, R. R.	Non-Refillable Bottle	May 2, 1899	624,092
Rhodes, J. B.	Water Closets	Dec. 19, 1899	639,290
Richardson, A. C.	Hame Fastener	Mar. 14, 1882	255,022
Richardson, A. C.	Churn	Feb. 17, 1891	446,470
Richardson, A. C.	Casket Lowering Device	Nov. 13, 1894	529,311
Richardson, A. C.	Insect Destroyer	Feb. 28, 1899	620,362
Richardson, A. C.	Bottle	Dec. 12, 1899	638,811
Richardson, W. H.	Cotton Chopper	June 1, 1886	343,140
Richardson, W. H.	Child's Carriage	June 18, 1889	405,599
Richardson, W. H.	Child's Carriage	June 18, 1889	405,600
Richey, C. V.	Car Coupling	June 15, 1897	584,650
Richey, C. V.	Railroad Switch	Aug. 3, 1897	587,657
Richey, C. V.	Railroad Switch	Oct. 26, 1897	592,448
Richey, C. V.	Fire Escape Bracket	Dec. 28, 1897	596,427
Richey, C. V.	Combined Hammock and Stretcher	Dec. 13, 1898	615,907
Rickman, A. L.	Overshoe	Feb. 8, 1898	598,816
Ricks, J.	Horseshoe	Mar. 30, 1886	338,781
Ricks, J.	Overshoes for Horses	June 6, 1899	626,245
Rillicux, N.	Sugar Refiner (Evaporating Pan)	Dec. 10, 1846	4,879
Robinson, E. R.	Casting Composite	Nov. 23, 1897	594,286

Inventor	Invention	Date	Patent
Robinson, E. R.	Electric Railway Trolley	Sep. 19, 1893	505,370
Robinson, J. H.	Life Saving Guards for Locomotives	Mar. 14, 1899	621,143
Robinson, J. H.	Life Saving Guards for Street Cars	Apr. 25, 1899	623,929
Robinson, J.	Dinner Pail	Feb. 1, 1887	356,852
Romain, A.	Passenger Register	Apr. 23, 1889	402,035
Ross, A. L.	Runner for Stops	Aug. 4, 1896	565,301
Ross, A. L.	Bag Closure	June 7, 1898	605,343
Ross, A. L.	Trousers Support	Nov. 28, 1899	638,068
Ross, J.	Bailing Press	Sep. 5, 1899	632,539
Roster, D. N.	Feather Curler	Mar. 10, 1896	556,166
Ruffin, S.	Vessels for Liquids and Manner of Sealing	Nov. 20, 1899	737,603
Russell, L. A.	Guard Attachment for Beds	Aug. 13, 1895	544,381
Sampson, G. T.	Sled Propeller	Feb. 17, 1885	312,388
Sampson, G. T.	Clothes Drier	June 7, 1892	476,416
Scottron, S. R.	Adjustable Window Cornice	Feb. 17, 1880	224,732
Scottron, S. R.	Cornice	Jan. 16, 1883	270,851
Scottron, S. R.	Pole Tip	Sep. 31, 1886	349,525
Scottron, S. R.	Curtain Rod	Aug. 30, 1892	481,720
Scottron, S. R.	Supporting Bracket	Sep. 12, 1893	505,008
Shanks, S. C.	Sleeping Car Berth Register	July 21, 1897	587,165
Shewcraft, F.	Letter Box	Detroit, Michigan	
Shorter, D. W.	Feed Rack	May 17, 1887	363,089
Smith, J. W.	Improvement in Games	Apr. 17, 1900	647,887
Smith, J. W.	Lawn Sprinkler	May 4, 1897	581,785
Smith, J. W.	Lawn Sprinkler	Mar. 22, 1898	601,065
Smith, P. D.	Potato Digger	Jan. 21, 1891	445,206
Smith, P. D.	Grain Binder	Feb. 23, 1892	469,279
Snow & Johns	Linament	Oct. 7, 1890	437,728
Spears, H.	Portable Shield for Infantry	Dec. 27, 1870	110,599
Spikes, R. B.	Combination Milk Bottle Opener/Bottle Cover	June 29, 1926	1,590,557
Spikes, R. B.	Method and Apparatus for Obtaining Average Samples and Temperature of Tank Liquids	Oct. 27, 1931	1,828,753
Spikes, R. B.	Automatic Gear Shift	Dec. 6, 1932	1,889,814

Inventor	Invention	Date	Patent
Spikes, R. B.	Transmission and Shifting Thereof	Nov. 28, 1933	1,936,996
Spikes, R. B.	Self-Locking Rack for Billiard Cues	around 1910	not found
Spikes, R. B.	Automatic Shoe Shine Chair	around 1939	not found
Spikes, R. B.	Multiple Barrell Machine Gun	around 1940	not found

(Some patents are not included here because of current litigation; or because they were so basic in nature that redesigning and refiling procedures are now in process.)

Inventor	Invention	Date	Patent
Standard, J.	Oil Stove	Oct. 29, 1889	413,689
Standard, J.	Refrigerator	July 14, 1891	455,891
Stewart & Johnson	Metal Bending Machine	Dec. 27, 1887	375,512
Stewart, E. W.	Punching Machine	May 3, 1887	362,190
Stewart, E. W.	Machine for Forming Vehicle Sear Bars	Mar. 22, 1887	373,698
Stewart, T. W.	Mop	June 13, 1893	499,402
Stewart, T. W.	Station Indicator	June 20, 1893	499,895
Sutton, E. H.	Cotton Cultivator	Apr. 7, 1874	149,543
Sweeting, J. A.	Device for Rolling Cigarettes	Nov. 30, 1897	594,501
Sweeting, J. A.	Combined Knife and Scoop	June 7, 1898	605,209
Taylor, B. H.	Rotary Engine	Apr. 23, 1878	202,888
Taylor, B. H.	Slide Valve	July 6, 1897	585,798
Temple, L.	Toggle Harpoon	1848, "Eyewitness, Black History"	
Thomas, S. E.	Waste Trap	Oct. 16, 1883	286,746
Thomas, S. E.	Waste Trap for Basins, Closets, Etc.	Oct. 4, 1887	371,107
Thomas, S. E.	Casting	July 31, 1888	386,941
Thomas, S. E.	Pipe Connection	Oct. 9, 1888	390,821
Toliver, G.	Propeller for Vessels	Apr. 28, 1891	451,086
Tregoning & Latimer	Globe Supporter for Electric Lamps	Mar. 21, 1882	255,212
Walker, P.	Machine for Cleaning Seed Cotton	Feb. 16, 1897	577,153
Walker, P.	Bait Holder	Mar. 8, 1898	600,241
Waller, J. N.	Shoemaker's Cabinet or Bench	Feb. 3, 1880	224,253
Washington, W.	Corn Husking Machine	Aug. 14, 1883	283,173
Watkins, Isaac	Scrubbing Frame	Oct. 7, 1890	437,849
Watts, J. R.	Bracket for Miners' Lamp	Mar. 7, 1893	493,137
West, E. H.	Weather Shield	Sep. 5, 1899	632,385

| Woods, G. T. | Electric Railway | May 26, 1903 | 729,481 |
| Wormley, J. | Life Saving Apparatus | May 24, 1881 | 242,091 |

Inventor	Invention	Date	Patent
West, J. W.	Wagon	Oct. 18, 1870	108,419
White, D. L.	Extension Steps for Cars	Jan. 12, 1897	574,969
White, J. T.	Lemon Squeezer	Dec. 8, 1896	572,849
Williams, C.	Canopy Frame	Feb. 2, 1892	468,280
Williams, J. P.	Pillow Sham Holder	Oct. 10, 1899	634,784
Winn, Frank	Direct Acting Steam Engine	Dec. 4, 1888	394,047
Winters, J. B.	Fire Escape Ladder	May 7, 1878	203,517
Winters, J. R.	Fire Escape Ladder Apr. 8, 1879	214,224	
Woods, G. T.	Steam Boiler Furnace	June 3, 1884	299,894
Woods, G. T.	Telephone Transmitter	Dec. 2, 1884	308,876
Woods, G. T.	Apparatus/Transmission Messages by Electricity	Apr. 7, 1885	315,368
Woods, G. T.	Relay Instrument	June 7, 1887	364,619
Woods, G. T.	Polarized Relay	July 5, 1887	366,192
Woods, G. T.	Electro Mechanical Brake	Aug. 16, 1887	368,265
Woods, G. T.	Telephone System and Apparatus	Oct. 11, 1887	371,241
Woods, G. T.	Electro Magnetic Brake Apparatus	Oct. 18, 1887	371,655
Woods, G. T.	Railway Telegraphy	Nov. 15, 1887	373,383
Woods, G. T.	Induction Telegraph System	Nov. 29, 1887	373,915
Woods, G. T.	Overhead Conducting System/Electric Railway	May 29, 1888	383,844
Woods, G. T.	Electro-Motive Railway System	June 26, 1888	385,034
Woods, G. T.	Runnel Construction for Electric Railway	July 17, 1888	386,282
Woods, G. T.	Galvanic Battery	Aug. 14, 1888	387,839
Woods, G. T.	Railway Telegraphy	Aug. 28, 1888	388,803
Woods, G. T.	Automatic Safety Cut-Out for Electric Circuits	Jan 1, 1889	395,533
Woods, G. T.	Electric Railway System	Nov. 10, 1891	463,020
Woods, G. T.	Electric Railway Conduit	Nov. 21, 1893	509,065
Woods, G. T.	System of Electrical Distribution	Oct. 13, 1896	569,443
Woods, G. T.	Amusement Apparatus	Dec. 19, 1899	639,692
Woods, G. T.	Electric Railway	Jan. 29, 1901	667,110
Woods, G. T.	Electric Railway System	July 9, 1901	678,086
Woods, G. T.	Regulate/Control Electrical Translating Devices	Sep. 3, 1901	681,768
Woods, G. T.	Electric Railway	Nov. 19, 1901	687,098
Woods, G. T.	Automatic Air Brake	June 10, 1902	701,981
Woods, G. T.	Electric Railway System	Jan. 13, 1903	718,183

Inventor	Invention	Date	Patent
Woods, G. T.	Electric Railway	May 26, 1903	729,481
Wormley, J.	Life Saving Apparatus	May 24, 1881	242,091

Bibliography

American Council of Learned Societies *A guide to Documents in the National Archives for Negro Studies.* Washington, D.C., 1947.

Arons, Stephen *Compelling Belief* McGraw-Hill, 1983

Begeman, Myron L. *Manufacturing Processes* Wiley, 1952.

Bennett, Jr., Lerone *Before the Mayflower* Johnson, 1962.

Collins, Marva & Tamarkin, Civia. *Marva Collins' Way* J. P. Tarcher Inc., 1982.

Cross, Theodore L *Black Capitalism* Atheneum, 1969.

Gilder, George *The Spirit of Enterprise* Simon and Schuster, 1984.

Herkimer, Herbert *The Engineer's Illustrated Thesaurus* Chemical Publishing Co., 1952.

Katz, William L *Eyewitness, The Negro in American History* Pitman, 1967; also, *Teachers Guide to American Negro History*

Ploski and Brown *The Negro Almanac* Bellwether, 1967.

Production Handbook Ronald Press, (any recent edition)

Rodriguez, Richard *Hunger of Memory* Godine, 1982.

Sowell, Thomas *Black Education - Myths and Tragedies* McKay, 1972.

Sowell, Thomas *Civil Rights: Rhetoric or Reality?* Morrow, 1984.

Sowell, Thomas *A Conflict of Visions* Morrow, 1987.

Sowell, Thomas *The Economics and Politics of Race* Morrow, 1983.

Sowell, Thomas *Ethnic America* Basic Books, 1981.

Sowell, Thomas *Markets and Minorities* Basic Books, 1981.

Williams, Walter *The State Against Blacks* McGraw-Hill, 1982.

The foremost authority in the field is Dr. John Hope Franklin, writer of the LIFE Magazine series on Black history. Professor Franklin, a Black man, is Chairman of the University of Chicago History Department; and also Chairman of the Fulbright Board. A Harvard Ph.D. and formerly Pitt professor of American history at Cambridge, his material may be considered as fundamental to any integrated structuring of the "Black Scene."

Patent and Invention Index

Printed in the United States
110446LV00004B/142-231/P

9 780981 683805